AF600429

THE CATHOLIC UNIVERSITY OF AMERICA
CANON LAW STUDIES
No. 222

COMPARATIVE LAW, ECCLESIASTICAL AND CIVIL, IN LITHUANIAN CONCORDAT

A STUDY WITH HISTORICAL NOTES

BY
JOSEPH PRUNSKIS, J.C.L.
Priest of the Diocese of Panevėžys, Lithuania

A DISSERTATION
Submitted to the Faculty of the School of Canon Law of the Catholic University of America in Partial Fulfillment of the Requirements for the Degree of
DOCTOR OF CANON LAW

THE CATHOLIC UNIVERSITY OF AMERICA PRESS
WASHINGTON, D. C.
1945

NIHIL OBSTAT:

EDUARDUS G. ROELKER, S.T.D., J.C.D.
Censor Deputatus
Washingtonii, D. C., die 7 Maii, 1945.

IMPRIMATUR:

MICHAEL J. CURLEY, D.D.,
Archiepiscopus Baltimorensis-Washingtonensis.

PRINTED IN THE UNITED STATES OF AMERICA
BY THE WATKINS PRINTING CO., BALTIMORE

TO MY FATHER

who always encouraged me to higher studies
and who died in exile in Siberia
before seeing the realization of his hopes.

TABLE OF CONTENTS

FOREWORD

Hardly any country has suffered so much during World War II as Catholic Lithuania. Three devastating occupations followed one another: Russian (1940-1941), German (1941-1944), and again Russian (1944-).

Huge armies of great powers, advancing and retreating, fought many cruel, destructive battles on her soil and traversed the fields and meadows of this peaceful nation of peasants.

Hundreds of thousands of Lithuanians are now in exile or in refuge. Such is the lot of the author of the present work. He considers that by preparing a study concerning the juridical conditions of the public religious life of Lithuania, as expressed in the Concordat, he will serve the cause of the Church and the country of Lithuania.

In the introduction to this work the author presents further reasons for the study of the legal norms of Lithuania, gives a review of the changes in the Constitution of that country and makes observations on the present status of the Lithuanian Concordat.

The work is divided into two sections. In the first part of the study are collected the main facts concerning Lithuania, and a review of the historical, political, and juridical conditions which led to the conclusion of the Concordat is presented.

The purpose of the second and main part of this work is to compare the stipulations of the Concordat, on the one hand, with the norms of the Code of Canon Law and with the principles of Ecclesiastical Public Law, and, on the other hand, with the latest Constitution of independent Lithuania as well as with the other laws and decrees of the Government.

The author feels greatly indebted to the professors of the School of Canon Law of the Catholic University of America for their generous helpfulness and kind guidance.

The author expresses his gratitude to those colleagues of the same University who helped to prepare the English copy, and sincerely thanks the many generous Lithuanians of the United States who, by their wholehearted support, enabled him to enjoy the privilege of being a student at the *Alma Mater* of the Catholics of America.

Chapter I

INTRODUCTION

1. Importance of the Question

The bloodshed of World War II, together with its occupations, deportations, and concentration camps, reminds us that in many countries justice is being trampled under foot. As His Excellency, the Apostolic Delegate to the United States, Archbishop Amleto G. Cicognani so eloquently expresses it, "Rights are being taken away while the whole world resounds with the praises of liberty." [1]

The longing for justice is great, because "without justice the state is nothing but organized robbery and the law of nations nothing but the law of destruction of the weak." [2]

After the present war, we may look for a period of cultural, economic, political and juridical reconstruction. Consequently, studies of juridical systems, even of unobserved treaties, will bring forward material that may contribute towards the evolving of new legal norms for some countries. As a famous jurist and journalist of Vatican City writes:

> The study of these diplomatic texts at this date is very much the study of something from which life has departed; yet it has advantages analogous to those of an autopsy; by furnishing information as to the causes of death, it may teach us something about the conditions of life.[3]

The comparative study of the principles of ecclesiastical and civil law as embodied in the Lithuanian Concordat is interesting

[1] Preface to the English version of Guido Gonella's book *A World to Reconstruct* (translated by L. Bouscaren, Milwaukee: The Bruce Publishing Company, 1944), p. xiii.

[2] Christopher Dawson, *The Judgment of the Nations* (New York: Sheed and Ward, 1942), p. 146.

[3] G. Gonella, *A World to Reconstruct,* p. 215.

from many viewpoints. Lithuania is a meeting point of two different civilizations, Western and Eastern.[4]

One can naturally expect to find that each has had its influence on Lithuanian juridical life, and hence Lithuania's legal system offers rather interesting subject-matter for study.

The legal life of Lithuania was developing in its own way, though under the shadow of two larger neighbors with growing totalitarian tendencies, Russia and Germany; yet all these and other cold winds from foreign countries did not hinder Lithuania from concluding a concordat, one of the best in the pre-war era (World War II) and one deserving of sincere praise from internationally known jurists.[5]

Lithuania deserves, then, our attention. It is, as His Holiness, Pope Pius XII, confirmed, the last Catholic stronghold in the northernmost part of Europe.[6]

The concordat which Lithuania concluded in 1927 is Lithuania's first and only complete treaty with the Holy See. It is a perfect example of one of the agreements completed in the great

[4] On the peculiar position of Lithuania there is a profound study written by the Lithuanian philosopher St. Šalkauskis: *Sur les Confins de deux Mondes.* Essai synthétique sur le problème de la Civilisation Nationale en Lithuanie (Berne: Bureau de Presse Lithuanien "Lietuva").

[5] E. g., F. M. Cappello writes: "Sollemnis conventio inter S. Sedem et Lithuaniae rempublicam die 27 sept. 1927 inita, summis laudibus extollenda est. Sane libertas et independentia Ecclesiae, eius iura divinitus accepta, relationes inter sacerdotium et imperium, secundum catholicam doctrinam, perspicue enuntiantur sollemnique pacti sanctitate et inviolabilitate firmantur. Complura in isto concordato reperiuntur, quae in ceteris pactis conventis desiderantur quaeque in maximam utilitatem tum religionis, tum reipublicae profecto cedunt." — "De Natura Concordatorum"—*Jus Pontificium,* VIII (1928), 15. *Jus Pontificium* hereafter abbreviated as *JP.*

[6] Allocutio *Heureux est pour Nous,* 18 oct., 1939: "Avant-poste septentional de la catholicité."—*Acta Apostolicae Sedis* (*AAS*), XXXI (1939), 611.

The allocution was made in reply to the Homage of the new Lithuanian Minister, Stanislaus Girdvainis.

era of concordats following World War I during the pontificate of Pius XI.[7]

It may be that the Lithuanian Concordat, together with others similar to it, will be a pattern for concordats during the coming period of world reconstruction after this cruel cataclysm.[8]

One's first desire, however, would be to see this treaty in full force in Lithuania itself. May she be delivered in the near future from occupation, and restored as a free, independent nation.[9]

2. Evolution of the Basic Law of Lithuania

Although the fundamental norms of the Ecclesiastical Law (Code, *Jus Publicum Ecclesiasticum*) and the norms of the Lithuanian Concordat have remained unchanged in the post-war period, the basic Law of Lithuania has undergone a sub-

[7] A. Ottaviani concludes his study of the Lithuanian Concordat ("Concordatum Lithuanicum"—*Apollinaris,* I [1928], 149) with the following words: "Satis igitur constare videtur, Concordatum Lithuanicum praeclarum exhibere exemplum illius concordiae quae vigere potest inter ecclesiasticam et civilem potestatem in Statu catholico . . . ".

[8] F. M. Cappello ("De Natura Concordatorum"—*JP,* VIII [1928], 18 says: "Vehementissime optandum est, ut omnia Gubernia, exemplum praeclarissimum reipublicae Lithuaniae secuta, Ecclesiae catholicae iura divinitus accepta eiusque libertatem et independentiam plane agnoscant eaque sancte religioseque custodire publica pactorum fide interposita promittant. Quot bona sacerdotio et imperio, religioni nempe et animorum concordiae ipsique publicae incolumitati ac prosperitati inde obventura sperare licebit!"

[9] In this connection one may well recall the words of the Apostolic Message, *Allorchè Fummo,* July 28, 1915, to the peoples at war and their rulers: "Remember that Nations do not die; humbled and oppressed, they chafe under the yoke imposed upon them, preparing a renewal of the combat, and passing down from generation to generation a mournful heritage of hatred and revenge. Why not from this moment weigh with serene mind the rights and lawful aspirations of the peoples? Why not initiate with a good will an exchange of views, directly or indirectly, with the object of holding in due account, within the limits of possibility, those rights and aspirations, and thus succeed in putting an end to the monstrous struggle, as has been done under other similar circumstances?"—Official English Version, *AAS,* VII (1915), 376.

stantial evolution. The Lithuanian Concordat was concluded when the Constitution of 1922 was still in force. That Constitution was framed by the men who fought against the oppression of the Czars and who were imprisoned and even sent into exile by them. After such a difficult struggle for liberty these patriots aspired to create a New Lithuania in which would prevail the same democratic spirit and freedom as existed in Switzerland, France, Sweden, and the United States. They were familiar with the conditions of these countries, for in the difficult days of persecution many of them sought refuge in these strongholds of liberty and democracy.

Moreover, in the Constituent Assembly, the purpose of which was to frame a new Constitution, the Catholic party (Christian Democrats) had a clear majority, that is, 59 seats out of 112.[10]

Naturally, the Lithuanian Constitution, accepted by the Constituent Assembly on August 1, 1922, was a basic law of liberty and democracy, devoting much attention to religious freedom.[11]

The entire spirit of the Constitution is well illustrated in the Preamble:

> In the name of Almighty God, the Lithuanian Nation, gratefully mindful of the glorious deeds of her sons and their noble sacrifices made to free their fatherland, having reconstituted her independent State, and desiring to establish for her independent life a firm democratic

[10] For the composition of Lithuanian diets (*Seimas*) see E. J. Harrison, *Lithuania* (London: Hazell, Watson and Viney, LD, 1928), p. 225.

[11] It was promulgated in *Vyriausybės Žinios,* No. 100 (1922), 1-8. *Vyriausybės Žinios*—The News of Government, official paper for promulgating laws, cited hereafter as *VŽ*.

In the Library of Congress (Washington, D. C.) there is a typed copy of an English translation of the Lithuanian Constitution. The copy was given to the Library by the Lithuanian Legation.

The official text of the English translation, which will be used in this study, is reprinted in M. W. Graham's book *New Governments of Eastern Europe* (New York: Henry Holt and Co., 1927), pp. 720-735. In this book Graham has a valuable survey of the political history of Lithuania, illustrated by a skillfully planned chart.

> base, to create conditions for the establishment of right and justice, and to assure to all her citizens equality, freedom, and welfare, and proper State protection for the work and morals of her people, through her duly authorized representatives formally convened as the Constituent Assembly, on the first day of August, 1922, adopted this the Constitution of the State of Lithuania.

The Constitution proclaims that the sovereign Government of the State shall be vested in the people (section 1), that all citizens are equal before the law (section 10), and that the person of the citizen and his home shall be inviolable (sections 11 and 12). The Constitution also guarantees secrecy of correspondence (section 14), freedom of speech (section 15), freedom to form societies and associations (section 16); and strong power of representation of the nation, called *Seimas* (sections 22-39).[12]

The Constitution's regulations concerning religion and other matters, treated later in the Concordat, are as follows:

> Section 10. All citizens of Lithuania, men and women, are equal before the law. No special privileges can be given to, nor shall the rights of citizens be restricted because of race, creed, or nationality.
>
> Section 13. Citizens shall have the right of freedom of religious belief and conscience.
>
> The belonging to any religion or the profession of one's convictions shall not form the basis for justification of an offense or for refusing to perform public duties.

[12] One of the leading jurists of Lithuania, the Rector of the University of Kaunas, M. Roemeris, writes about this constitution: "Die alte Verfassung von 1922 stellte ein streng zum Ausdruck gebrachtes parlamentarisches System nach französischem Muster dar, wonach das dem Seim verantwortliche Ministerkabinett des Vertrauens der Seimmehrheit bedürfe und bei Entziehung dieses Vertrauens zurückzutreten hatte (Art. 59 der Verf. vom 1922)."—*Die Verfassungsreform Litauens vom Jahre 1928,* Quellen und Studien. Abteilung: Recht, 7. Heft (München: Osteuropa-Institut in Breslau, 1930), p. 30.

Section 80. Religious education in schools shall be compulsory, with the exception of schools established for children whose parents do not belong to any religious organization. Religion shall be taught in accordance with the requirements of those religious organizations to which the students belong.

Section 82. Private religious schools, provided they comply with the minimum of the program fixed by law, shall receive from the State Treasury for the purpose of education that part of the budget appropriation which shall correspond to the number of Lithuanian citizens and students belonging to such religion which shall conduct such schools and education.

Section 83. The State recognizes the equal right of all religious organizations existing in Lithuania to administer their affairs in accordance with the requirements of their canons or statutes, to freely publish their religious doctrines and to practice their cult ceremonies, to establish and manage their cult buildings, schools, educational and charitable institutions, to establish convents, religious congregations and fraternities, to impose upon their members dues for the needs of the religious organizations, and to acquire and manage personal and real property.

Religious organizations shall possess the rights of legal entities in the State.

Spiritual advisers are relieved from military obligations.

Section 85. Birth, marriage or death certificates,[13] made by the faithful before their spiritual advisers, if they comply with the form determined by law, shall have legal force in Lithuania, and citizens shall not be compelled to repeat such acts in another institution.

[13] In the translation of the Lithuanian Legation (cf. footnote No. 11) instead of "certificates" is found the word "acts," which more correctly translates the Lithuanian word, "aktai," as found in the original text of the Constitution.

Section 85. The laws shall protect Sundays and other holidays recognized by the State as days of rest and spiritual need.

Section 87. Soldiers shall be granted leave to attend to their religious duties.

Persons in hospitals, jails, and other public institutions shall be given the opportunity to attend to their religious duties.

A. Giannini was right when, after giving a summary of the Lithuanian Constitution, he wrote that hardly any other state accords such freedom to the Church as does Lithuania.[14]

But the life of such a democratic Constitution was not to last very long. On December 17, 1926, following an uprising, the then existing Lithuanian government was overthrown and in its place a nationalistic government gradually came to power.[15]

Nationalists, however, did not have the support of the majority of the people. To keep the country under control, the government, headed by President A. Smetona, decided to proclaim a new Constitution which would strengthen the power of the President and reduce the power of the *Seimas* (Diet). It was promulgated on May 15, 1928.[16]

In this new Constitution the hegemony was transferred from the *Seimas* to the Government, and then to the President.[17]

[14] "Forse . . . in nessun altro Paese vi è una così grande larghezza da parte dello Stato verso le organizzazione confessionali . . . "—A. Giannini, *I Concordati Postbellici* (Milano: Vita e Pensiero, 1929), p. 210.

[15] It cannot be denied that some reforms of political life in Lithuania were really necessary. For example, there was serious division among the various political parties regarding their attitude towards religion. Political campaigns and agitations accompanying them frequently brought about an undesirable effect on the morale and spirit of the country, due to attacks unjustly leveled against the Church.

[16] *VŽ,* No. 275 (1928), 1-6. The English text prepared by officials of the Ministry of Foreign Affairs of Lithuania is published in Harrison's book, *Lithuania,* pp. 365-377. This translation iwll be used in the present study.

[17] Cf. M. Römer, *Die Verfassung Litauens vom Jahre 1928,* p. 34: "Der litauische Präsident verfügt über derartige verfassungsmäszige Mittel,

The President was to be elected by special representatives of the Nation, not by the *Seimas,* for a term of seven years (Sect. 43). He could be reëlected without any restrictions, and the new Constitution did not give the power to the *Seimas* to dismiss a President.

The Constitutional reform was commented upon by jurists as a step toward an authoritative form of government.[18]

The sections about religion, cults, education, and freedom of associations remained without any substantial changes. These

dasz er seine persönliche Macht sogar bis zur Diktatur ausdehnen kann, jedoch nur under der Bedingung der befristeten Seimauflösung. Indem er das Kabinett seiner Person völlig unterordnet und sich gleichzeitig von den Fesseln des Parlementarismus durch Auflösung des Seims befreit, bezahlt er dieses aber mit seiner Abhängigkeit von einem anderen, weit stärkeren Machtfaktor—vom Volke (die Wählermasse des Seims)."

[18] "Indubbiamente alle vestali delle costituzioni ultrademocratiche le accenate riforme appariscono dettate da spirito antidemocratico e rappresentano un passo indietro sui democraticissimi ordinamenti del 1922. Non si può negare che ciò sia vero. Ma non c'è de compiacersene. Se, dopo sei anni di dure esperienze, si sono eliminati gli eccessi democratici, arginati i pericoli di un onnipotente parlamentarismo affaristico, ciò costituisce un atto di coraggio e di sana volutazione dei bisogni nazionali. Nè si può negare seriamente, io ritengo, che, anche eliminati gli eccessi, la costituzione lituana continui ad essere una delle più democratiche del mondo." A. Giannini, "La Revisione della Costituzione Lituana"—*L'Europa Orientale,* IX (1929), 412.

"Wobec braku w nowej konstytucji przepisów o kontroli działalności organów administracji, przepisy o swobodach obywatelskich, nawet w wypadku pełnego zrealizowania ich w ustawach szscegółowych, pozostaną bez sankcji sądowej martwą literą lub conajwyżej normą zawislą w swem wykonaniu od swobodnego uznania i samovoli władz administracyjnych. Zbliży to administrację Litwy do typu organizacji administracyjnej w państwach policyjnych, oddali zaśię stanowczo od typu państwa praworządnego, które już ku końcowi ubiegłego stulecia stało się prawie powszechne w Europie." Art. Miller, *Nowa Konstytucja Państwa Litewskiego* (Warszawa: F. Hoesicki, 1930), p. 19.

See also N. Turchi, "La Costituzione del 1922. La Modificazione del 1928" in his book *La Lituania nella Storia e nel Presente* (Roma: Istituto per L'Europa Orientale, 1933), pp. 92-99.

sections were for the most part repeated *verbatim* from the former Constitution.

Art. 106 of the new Constitution stated:

> This Constitution comes into force from the date of its proclamation, but must be approved or disapproved by a referendum within ten years.

This gave the new Constitution a temporary, experimental character.[19]

Ten years later, the third Constitution was accepted by the Lithuanian Diet and was promulgated by the President on May 12, 1938.[20]

There was in this Constitution a further development of the authoritative form of the life of the State.[21] The Constitution of 1938 does not say that Lithuania is a democratic state, as the previous Constitutions had said in the first section. The power now is even more concentrated in the hands of the President. He is not responsible for acts which emanate from his power. Even with regard to personal crimes and transgressions he is not subject to punishment as long as he is in power.[22]

[19] Cf. A. Giannini, "La Revisione della Costituzione Lituana" — *L'Europa Orientale,* IX (1929), 408-409: "L'art. 106 stabilisce che la nuova costituzione entra in vigore il giorno della sua promulgazione (cioè 25 maggio 1928, come abbiamo detto) ma essa non ha carattere definitivo. Non più tardi di 10 anni dalla sua promulgazione deve essere confermata per referendum nazionale. Può dunque essere confermata, ma per sua natura è considerata come passabile di esperimento; esperimento, per altro, che si vuole serio ed efficace per dare al popolo gli elementi necessari e sufficienti per decidere della sua bontà, con matura riflessione e convinzione."

[20] *VŽ,* No. 608 (1938), 237-245.

[21] A more detailed discussion of the Constitution of 1938, especially concerning religion, the right of meeting and organizing, schools and education, will be given in the second part of this study, when a comparison between the articles of the Concordat and the principles of the new Constitution will be made.

[22] Sect. 73: "Respublikos Prezidentas neatsako už savo galios veiksmus. Už kitus veiksmus respublikos Prezidentas negali būti šaukiamas atsakyti, ligi vadovauja Valstybei."—*VŽ,* No. 608 (1938), 240.

The President of the Republic appoints and dismisses the Prime Minister and other Ministers.[23]

The representatives of the nation (the *Seimas*) no longer have the power to dismiss Ministers as they had in the Constitution of 1922, according to section 59.[24]

There remained, however, in the Constitution of 1938 sufficient provisions for basic liberties, but the people and their representatives were destitute of means of control, since almost everything depended upon the good will of the Government, especially on that of the President.

3. Is the Lithuanian Concordat Still in Force?

Lithuania now is occupied by the Bolsheviks. This is the second Bolshevistic occupation. The first occupation continued from June 15, 1940, until June 23, 1941.[25]

During the second occupation the Bolsheviks are directing the public and private life of Lithuanians according to the same pattern as before. The Lithuanian American Information Center has issued this bulletin:

> The Committee of the Lithuanian Communist Party met at Vilnius and decided, according to the *Swiss News Agency,* to restore all the Soviet laws and decrees of the Bolshe-

[23] Sect. 97: "Ministrą Pirmininką ir jo pristatymu Ministro Pirmininko Pavaduotoją ir kitus Ministrus skiria ir atleidžia Respublikos Prezidentas."—*VŽ,* No. 608 (1938), 242.

[24] "The Ministers must have the confidence of the *Seimas.* If the *Seimas* shall directly declare want of confidence in them, the Cabinet of Ministers and each Minister must resign."

[25] This dark period of Lithuanian history is fairly well described in the book *Timeless Lithuania* (Chicago: Amerlith Press, 1943), written by the former Envoy Extraordinary and Minister Plenipotentiary of the United States to Lithuania, Owen J. C. Norem. This book is well written, but must be read cautiously, since Norem, a Protestant minister, at times misunderstood the life and works of the Catholic groups in Lithuania.

Cf. also the book of K. Pakštas, *The Lithuanian Situation* (Chicago: Lithuanian Cultural Institute, 1941), pp. 8-58.

vik period during the summer of 1940 to the summer of 1941. In addition, all Soviet and Party courts and institutions will be re-established in all parts of Lithuania occupied by the Soviet army.[26]

What, then, is the Soviet attitude towards the Lithuanian Concordat? In a trustworthy report received from Lithuania and published in the United States of America it is stated:

> The Concordat was denounced on June 26, 1940, just ten days after the invasion by the Russians. On that day Papal Nuncio, Monsignor Centoz, was invited to the Foreign Office where he was rudely informed that a new "Soviet Lithuania" did not consider it necessary to maintain spiritual relations with the spiritual head of the Catholic Church. At the same time Monsignor Centoz was ordered to vacate his apartment within two days and to leave Lithuania before August 25, 1940.
>
> The Russians did not assign any other apartment to Monsignor Centoz in spite of his requests. Furthermore, they disregarded the Nuncio's diplomatic status and attempted to prevent the removal of his own furniture from his former apartment. His small bank account was sequestered by order of N. Pozdniakov, the Soviet Envoy to Lithuania, who overnight became an all-powerful Deputy-Chief of the Kremlin, second only to the special envoy, Dekanozov.[27]

A series of new decrees, directed against the Church, religion, and religious practices, was issued after the breaking of the Concordat: the Church was separated from the State;[28] subsidies and religious offices in public institutions were suppressed;[29] the

[26] *Žinių Santrauka*, No. 21 (1944), 1.

[27] A. Trakiškis, *The Situation of the Church and Religious Practices in Occupied Lithuania*, Part I. Under the Soviet Occupation, 1940-41 (New York: Lithuanian Bulletin, 1944), pp. 8-9.

[28] Art. 96 of the new Constitution of "Soviet Lithuania."—*VŽ*, No. 730 (1940), 657-663.

[29] *VŽ*, No. 713 (1940), 450.

Theological-Philosophical Faculty was closed;[30] private schools were liquidated;[31] all records of baptism, marriage, and death were taken away from the clergy;[32] civil marriage was introduced;[33] all religious instruction in schools was abolished;[34] lessons of Marxism-Leninism were introduced,[35] and orders were issued to terminate the activities of all Catholic and patriotic organizations. However, organizations pertaining to the Communistic Party and Freethinkers (in Lithuania they are atheists) were exempted from this order.[36]

During one year of occupation the Bolsheviks had killed fifteen Roman Catholic priests in Lithuania,[37] and exiled more than 40 thousand Lithuanians to Siberia, among them ten Roman Catholic priests.[38]

Hundreds upon hundreds of Lithuanians were killed in their own native land.[39]

It is difficult to speak about the existence of the Lithuanian Concordat when hardly any juridical order now exists in occupied Lithuania, and when the future existence of the nation itself is in great peril. The Lithuanian Concordat is denounced by the Soviets and, therefore, its legal force is suspended.

[30] *VŽ*, No. 720 (1940), 529.

[31] *VŽ*, No. 724 (1940), 603-604 and *VŽ*, No. 727 (1940), 640.

[32] *VŽ*, No. 725 (1940), 623-626.

[33] *VŽ*, No. 725 (1940), 619-623.

[34] *VŽ*, No. 727 (1940), 641.

[35] *VŽ*, No. 727 (1940), 642.

[36] Cf. A. Trakiškis, *The Situation of the Church and Religious Practices in Occupied Lithuania*, pp. 16-19.

[37] Cf. J. Prunskis, *Fifteen "Liquidated" Priests in Lithuania* (Chicago, 1943), pp. 3-15.

[38] Cf. J. Prunskis, *Bolševikų Kalėjime ir Sibiro Ištrėmime* (In the Bolshevistic Jails and in Exile of Siberia; Chicago: A. Gilis, 1943).

[39] Cf. J. Prunskis and S.Š., *Lietuva Nacių ir Bolševikų Vergijoje* (Lithuania under the Slavery of Nazism and Bolshevism; Chicago: A. L. R. K. Federacijos Cicagos Apskr. Spaudos Sekcijos Leidinys Nr. 1, 1944), pp. 16-27.

But this was done as an unjust, unilateral act by the party of the Soviets, who are only occupants of Lithuania. What the value of such an act is, may be judged from the authoritative word of Pope Pius IX when his Holiness condemned the proposition that secular power has the authority to denounce, to rescind, and to make void concordats.[40]

Pope Pius X in his Encyclical *Vehementer Nos*, February 11, 1906, speaking about the concordat of France, declared that no one party is entitled to dissolve a treaty.[41] And Pius XI in the Allocution *Con Grande*, December 24, 1938, stated:

> If in the case of the observance or non-observance of every bilateral pact, its interpretation cannot be usurped by one of the parties alone, much more must this hold true for an interpretation which has for its effect the releasing and freeing from every obligation.[42]

The breaking of agreements is contrary to International Law,[43]

[40] Syllabus errorum, prop. XLII: "Laica potestas auctoritatem habet rescindendi, declarandi ac faciendi irritas conventiones (vulgo Concordata) super iurium ad ecclesiasticam immunitatem pertinentium cum Sede Apostolica initas sine huius consensu, immo et ea reclamante." — *Acta Sanctae Sedis* (*ASS*), III (1867), 172; H. Denzinger, et Cl. Bannwart, et J. Umberg, *Enchiridion Symbolorum, Definitionum et Declarationum de Rebus Fidei et Morum* (21-23 ed., Friburgi Brisgoviae: Herder, 1937), n. 1743; hereafter cited as H. Denzinger, *Enchiridion Symbolorum*.

[41] "Ista pactio eodem iure ac ceterae quae inter civitates fiunt regeretur, hoc est, iure gentium; ideoque dissolvi ab alterutro dumtaxat eorum qui pepigerunt, nequaquam posset."—*ASS*, XXXIX (1906), 7.

[42] Cf. translation in *The Catholic Mind;* see *Principles for Peace* (selections from Papal Documents, Leo XIII to Pius XII, edited for Bishops' Committee on the Pope's Peace Points, Washington, D. C.: National Catholic Welfare Conference, 1943), n. 1307.

Original Italian, *Civiltà Cattolica,* XC (1939), 85-86: " . . . se per ogni patto bilaterale e per la sua osservanza o non osservanza, l'interpretazione non può usurparsi da una parte sola, molto più deve questo valere per una interpretazione cosi risolutiva e liberativa da ogni impegno."

[43] Cf. H. Wagnon. *Concordats et Droit International,* Fondament, Élaboration, Valeur et Cessation du Droit Concordataire, Universitas Catholica Lovaniensis, Dissertationes ad gradum magistri in Facultate Theo-

and stands condemned by leading officials of states.[44] Moreover, since the Bolsheviks have occupied neutral Lithuania by force, they are not entitled to destroy the juridical order of the country.[45]

logica vel in Facultate Iuris Canonici consequendum conscriptae, Series II, Tomus 29 (Gembloux: J. Duculot, 1935), p. 281: "Ce principe de droit a été affirmé de façon solonnelle par les grandes puissances européennes dans une déclaration annexe aux Protocole de Londres de 1871: les plénipotentiaires d'Allemagne, d'Angleterre, d'Autriche, d'Italie, de Russie et de Turquie 'reconaissent que c'est un principe essentiel du droit des gens qu'aucune puissance ne puisse se libérer des engagements d'un traité ni en modifier les stipulations, qu'à la suite de l'assentiment des parties contractantes, au moyen d'une entente amicale'."

[44] Cordell Hull, at that time Secretary of the Department of State of the United States, Chairman of the American delegation at the Inter-American Conference for the Maintenance of Peace, in his opening address, on December 5, 1936, said: "Observance of understandings, agreements, and treaties between nations constitutes the foundation of international order. . . . If the solemn rights and obligations between nations are to be treated lightly or brushed aside, the nations of the world will head straight toward international anarchy and chaos."—C. Hull, *Opening Address to the Inter-American Conference for the Maintenance of Peace* (Washington, D. C.: Government Printing Office, 1936), p. 13.

C. J. Hambro, the President of the League of Nations Assembly and of the Norwegian Parliament, in his book *How to Win the Peace* (Philadelphia: J. B. Lippincott Company, 1942), p. 42, writes: " . . . if a promise means to one party a binding obligation, and to the other party a dope given an opponent; if a solemn declaration means to one party a sacred statement of facts or of a serious policy and no more than a bid in poker to the other party—no treaty in any known language is of any value to the old-fashioned party still fondly taking that a word is a word and a man a man, conceptions non-existent in the moral language of the other party. Any agreement signed by him will lay him open to assault, aggression, invasion, unspeakable oppression, tyranny, and cruelty."

[45] Cf. G. Gonnella, *A World to Reconstruct,* p. 165: "As regards occupied territories, positive international law makes the fact of occupation (which is not a change of sovereignty, and therefore does not suspend national laws or national tribunals) the basis of a series of rights and duties between the occupants and the populations of occupied territories. . . . When the territory occupied is neutral instead of enemy territory, the obligations of the occupying power are far more stringent."

The Soviets do not represent the Lithuanian nation, which, even after the denouncement of the Concordat by the Bolsheviks, still believes in the validity and the binding force of that treaty.[46] The Vatican does not recognize Soviet Lithuania. The Minister of Lithuania still remains at the Vatican, representing the free, independent country of Lithuania. Neither does the United States of America recognize the Soviet annexation of Lithuania. In Washington even now (1945) there is a Lithuanian Legation with a Minister representing Independent, but not Soviet Lithuania.[47]

[46] The author is in possession of a copy of the memorandum of the protest which, on October 13, 1942, was given by the Lithuanian bishops to the German occupational authorities. The bishops, protecting the rights of the Theological-Philosophical Faculty, invoke the Lithuanian Concordat, despite the fact that the Soviets had denounced it during their former occupation (1940-1941).

[47] After the occupational forces of the Red Army were settled in the Baltic States and after the sham "elections" of the "people's diet," were held, the Department of State of the United States Government issued the following statement on July 23, 1940: "During these past few days the devious processes whereunder the political independence and territorial integrity of the three small Baltic republics—Estonia, Latvia, and Lithuania—were to be deliberately annihilated by one of their more powerful neighbors, have been rapidly drawing to their conclusion.

From the day when the peoples of these republics first gained their independent and democratic form of government the people of the United States have watched their admirable progress in self-government with deep sympathetic interest.

The policy of this Government is universally known. The people of the United States are opposed to predatory activities no matter where they are carried on by force or by the threat of force. They are likewise opposed to any form of intervention on the part of one state, however powerful, in the domestic concerns of any other sovereign state, however weak.

These principles constitute the very foundations upon which the existing relationship between the 21 sovereign republics of the New World rests.

The United States will continue to stand by these principles, because of the conviction of the American people that unless the doctrine in which these principles are inherent once again governs the relations between nations, the rule of reason, of justice, and of law—in other words, the basis of modern civilization itself—cannot be preserved."—*The Department of State Bulletin,* III (1940), 48.

The hope that justice and the rights of oppressed nations will be restored brings a conviction that the suspension of the force of the Lithuanian Concordat is merely temporary.[48]

[48] About the postwar problems of the Baltic State see A. Bilmanis, *The Baltic States in Post-War Europe* (Washington, D. C.: Latvian Legation, 1944), pp. 3-30.

PART ONE

THE POLITICAL AND JURIDICAL SITUATION WHICH LED TO THE LITHUANIAN CONCORDAT

CHAPTER II

SOME INTERNAL AND INTERNATIONAL PROBLEMS OF NEW LITHUANIA

1. LAND AND NATION

Lithuania (Lietuva) is located on the south eastern shore of the Baltic Sea, between Latvia, Poland, and Germany. Lithuanians "are the autochthonous (at least for 4,000 years) inhabitants of the eastern shores of the Baltic Sea."[1]

The Lithuanian nation is one of the oldest in Europe, entirely different from the Slav and German; the Lithuanian language, which is derived from the *Primitive Indo-European,* is also one of the oldest in Europe, different from any other living European language, except Latvian.[2] Linguists find great similarity between the ancient Sanskrit and the modern Lithuanian.[3] The Lithuanian language is now spoken in everyday life by about 3,800,000 persons all over the world.[4]

[1] A. Bilmanis, *The Baltic States and the Baltic Sea* (Washington, D. C.: Latvian Legation, 1943), p. 9.

[2] Cf. A. Senn, *The Lithuanian Language* (Chicago: Lithuanian Cultural Institute, 1942), pp. 5-23.

[3] A. Senn, *op. cit.*, p. 5. In some universities, as, e.g., in Koenigsberg, the students of Sanskrit are advised to study the Lithuanian language, because this helps them to understand the "mother" language of many nations (Sanskrit).

Cf. A. Meillet, *Les Annales des Nationalités* (1913), p. 205: "Qui veut retrouver sur les lèvres des hommes un écho de se qu'a pu être la langue commune indo-européenne, va écouter les paysans lithuaniens d'aujourd'-hui." Cited from A. Viscont, *La Lithuanie Religieuse* (Paris: G. Cres & Cie., 1918), p. 15.

[4] A. Senn, *The Lithuanian Language*, p. 7.

The early religion of Lithuania was pagan, consisting in the adoration of the different gods and powers of nature. The Lithuanians believed in life after death. Their priests—*kriviai, vaidilos* —preached the need of hospitality, of friendship and of an exalted moral life.[5]

The Teutonic Knights, beginning with the thirteenth century, made many attempts to impose Christianity upon the Lithuanians by sword, but were not successful. However, the country received Christianity through Poland, at the end of the fourteenth century (1387).[6] The western part of Lithuania, Žemaitija (Samogitia), received Christianity at a later period, in 1413.[7]

The peak of the territorial expansion of Lithuania was reached in the fourteenth and fifteenth centuries, when the frontiers of the state extended from the Baltic to the Black Sea. This made Lithuania one of the largest states in Europe.[8] For many centuries Lithuania was able to resist the savage hordes of the Tartars and of other Asiatics,who had subjugated Moscow and were streaming to the western part of Europe. For more than two hundred years Lithuania fought the German *Drang nach Osten* by resisting the Teutonic Knights. Finally Lithuania became weaker and united with Poland: first, when a Lithuanian Dynasty ruled both countries (1430-1572), later, in 1569, when there was a formal Union with Poland (Union of Lublin).[9]

But internal discrepancies occasioned by the clinging to privi-

[5] Cf. A. Šapoka, *Lietuvos Istorija* (Kaunas Švietimo Ministerijos leidinys, 1936), pp. 34-37. This work is, up to the present, the best history of Lithuania, written in the Lithuanian language. In English there is the work of A. Jusaitis, *The History of the Lithuanian Nation and its present National Aspirations* (The Lithuanian Catholic Truth Society, 1918).

[6] Concerning the introduction of Christianity into Lithuania there is a study by S. Yla, *Krikščionybės Įvedimas Lietuvoje* (Kaunas: "Sakalas." 1938).

[7] The text of the bull establishing the diocese of Samogitia is reprinted in *JP*, IX (1929), 271-278. There are photostatic copies of the bull also (p. 273).

[8] Cf. K. Pakštas, *The Lithuanian Situation*, p. 5.

[9] Cf. A. Šapoka, *Lietuvos Istorija*, pp. 168-227.

leges and the furthering of selfishness on the part of the nobility (*szlachta*), debilitated the two united nations. As a result both were finally subjugated by Russia and Prussia. Disaster came in 1795; the greatest part of Lithuania was occupied by Russia, and the south western part, with the districts of Suvalkija and Klaipėda (Memel), was taken by the Germans.[10]

The Russian invaders began to "russianize" the Lithuanians. Seeing the great spirit of resistance on the part of Catholics, Orthodox Russia began to combat the Catholic Church in Lithuania. Many Catholic institutions were closed and their property confiscated.[11] Pope Leo XIII, affected by such atrocities, sent a letter to Alexander, Emperor of Russia at the time.[12] A Concordat with Russia in 1847 had remedied some evils [13] and the agreements in 1882 [14] and in 1907.[15] brought some alleviation, but it was not very considerable.

Even printing in Latin characters was forbidden to Lithuanians in 1865, because the Russians wanted them to accept the Russian alphabet, so that in due time they would use Russian literature and language. As a matter of fact, many continued to use Lithuanian books that were printed in Prussia and smuggled into Lithuania; others used Polish prayer books and literature.[16]

After World War I, when Germany was defeated and Russia had collapsed on account of revolution and civil. war, Lithuania on February 16, 1918 declared her independence, after 123 years

[10] A. Šapoka, *op. cit.,* p. 439.

[11] See *La Persécution de L'Eglise en Lithuanie,* traduction de Lescouer (Paris: Charles Douniol et Cie., 1873).

[12] *Principles for Peace,* n. 19-21.

[13] A. Mercati, *Raccolta di Concordati* (Roma: Tipografia Poliglotta Vaticana, 1919), pp. 751-765.

[14] Mercati, *op. cit.,* pp. 1016-1018.

[15] Mercati, *op. cit.,* 1097-1099.

[16] The fact that in view of these circumstances many Lithuanians had to use Polish literature is one of the reasons that some Lithuanians were imbued with the spirit of Polish culture.

of Russian occupation.[17] Russia, the former ruler of the country, renounced all her rights to Lithuania by the treaty signed at Moscow on July 12, 1920. Article I of the treaty states:

> Proceeding from the right, proclaimed by the Russian Socialist Federated Soviet Republic, of all nations to free self-determination up to their complete separation from the State into the composition of which they enter, Russia recognizes without reservation the sovereign rights and independence of the Lithuanian State, with all the juridical consequences arising from such recognition, and voluntarily and for all time abandons all the sovereign rights of Russia over the Lithuanian people and their territory.
>
> The fact of the past subjection of Lithuania to Russia does not impose on the Lithuanian nation and its territory any liabilities whatsoever towards Russia.[18]

One of the greatest accomplishments of Independent Lithuania was the agrarian reform brought about by the Minister of Agriculture, the Rev. M. Krupavičius, a Christian Democrat, with the support of other groups.[19]

In 1923, after the revolt of Klaipėda (Memel), that district was united with Lithuania. The problem of Vilnius (Vilna, Wilno), which was under Polish occupation, remained unsolved. After the collapse of Poland (1939), by a treaty with Russia,[20] Vilnius was given back to Lithuania. Lithuania, with the Klaipėda

[17] Photostatic copy of Declaration of Independence is in A. Šapoka's book *Lietuvos Istorija*, p. 544.

[18] P. Dailydė, *Lietuvos Sutartys su Svetimomis Valstybėmis.* Recueil des Traités Conclus par la Lithuanie avec les Pays Etrangers (2 vols., Kaunas: Užsienių Reikalų Ministerijos leidinys, 1930-1939), I, 30-52. Translation communicated by His Majesty's Foreign Office.—*League of Nations, Treaty Series,* III (1921), 122-123.

Cf. G. Rutenberg, "The Baltic States and the Soviet Union,"—*American Journal of International Law,* XXIX (1935), 598-615.

[19] A. Činikas, in 1937, wrote a thesis at the university of Nancy entitled *La Reforme Agraire en Lithuanie* (Nancy: V. Idoux, 1937).

[20] *VŽ,* No. 669 (1939), 636-642.

(Memel) territory and the Vilnius region (according to the Peace Treaty of July 12, 1920, with Russia) totaled 33,937 sq. mi.; the population of Lithuania, including the Klaipėda territory and the Vilnius region, was 3,032,863.

The percentage of Religions was as follows: Roman Catholic, 80.33%; Lutheran (Evangelical), 9.56%; Russian Orthodox, 2.62%; all other forms of Christianity, 0.08%; Hebrew, 7.30%; all other non-Christian bodies, 0.07%.

2. Lithuania and the Vatican

In the internal life of New Lithuania there soon arose a number of important juridical problems. In different parts of the country there were in force three different legal systems: the Russian *Сводъ Законовъ* in Lithuania Proper, the Prussian *Bürgerliches Gesetzbuch* in the Klaipėda (Memel) district, and the French *Code Napoléon* in Suvalkija.[22]

In the *Code Napoléon*,[23] and in the *Bürgerliches Gesetzbuch*[24] marriage legislation is more accommodated to the Prptestant way

[21] *Statistikos Biuletenis* (Bulletin of Statistics), No. 10 (1939), 1-3. Cf. A. Simutis, *The Economic Reconstruction of Lithuania after 1918* (New York: Columbia University Press, 1942), pp. 13-15.

[22] The French law was introduced by Napoleon when he conquered Prussia (1807) and created a duchy of Warsaw, which included the southeastern part of Lithuania, Suvalkija. Even after the power of Napoleon passed, the *Code Napoléon* remained in force in Suvalkija.—A. Šapoka, *Lietuvos Istorija*, p. 449.

About the earlier legal systems in Lithuania there is a study by A. Janulaitis, *Lietuvos Visuomenės ir Teisės Istorija* (Tilžė: Švietimo Ministerijos leidinys, 1920).

[23] Cf. Titre V: "Du Marriage."—*Code Napoléon* (édition originale et seule officielle, Paris: L'Imprimerie Impériale, 1810), pp. 36-73. Later this provision was changed by the Statute on Matrimony of March 16, 1836. See *Собранie Гражданскихъ Законовъ Губернiй Царства Польского* (Сапк-Петербургъ: Типографiя Второго Отдѣленiя Собственной Е. И. В. Канцелярiй, 1870), pp. 149-200.

[24] Viertes Buch: *Familienrecht*, Siebenter Titel: *Scheidung der Ehe.*—*Bürgerliches Gesetzbuch vom 18 August 1896 nebst Einführungsgesetz* (Berlin: J. Schweizer Verlag, 1914), pp. 471-478.

of life, and the *Сводъ Законовъ* favors the Orthodox Church, restricting the rights of Catholics.[25] But in Independent Lithuania, the majority of the people were Catholics and Catholicism was the state religion. Accordingly Lithuania, in planning to introduce the necessary changes in legislation, felt the need of getting in touch with the Head of the Catholic Church, the Pope.

There were also other reasons for seeking relations with the Vatican. According to the former agreements with the Czars in 1798,[26] 1847,[27] 1882,[28] and 1907,[29] the Lithuanian dioceses of Vilnius and Samogitia were under the jurisdiction of the metropolitan of Mohilev, and the diocese of Seinai was subject to the archdiocese of Warsaw.[30] This was very inconvenient, because Lithuania did not have any official relations with Poland, and the Archbishop of Mohilev was inaccessible on account of Soviet Russia's attitude towards the Church. Moreover, the prestige of the nation was affected by such a subjection of the Catholic Church of Lithuania to foreign countries against which she had had to fight so hard for her independence.

Many Lithuanians in the Vilnius section were under Polish administration. Lithuania at that time did not have diplomatic relations with Poland, and so, in order to insure the right of the Lithuanians of Vilnius to use their native language, at least in church, there remained only one way, and that was through the

[25] E. g., *Сводъ Законовъ Російской Имперій,* томъ X, частъ I: *Сводъ Законовъ Гражданскихъ и Положеніе о Казенныхъ Порядкахъ и Поставкахъ.* Изданіе 1914 года, ст. 65-75.

(This collection of laws will be cited hereafter as *Сводъ Законовъ,* Vol. X, part I) ; Cf. *Сводъ Законовъ Російской Имперій,* томъ XI, часть I. *Уставъ Духовныхъ Дѣлъ Иностранныхъ Вѣроисповѣданій.* Изданіе 1896 г., ст. 1-130.

(This second collection will be cited hereafter as *Сводъ Законовъ,* Vol. XI, part I).

[26] Mercati, *Raccolta di Concordati,* p. 538.

[27] *Op. cit.,* p. 751.

[28] *Op. cit.,* p. 1016.

[29] *Op. cit.,* p. 1096.

[30] Cf. Ottaviani. "Concordatum Lithuanicum"—*Apollinaris,* I (1928), 54.

Vatican. There were many other unsolved questions, e.g., in regard to the claims of the Church for property taken away by the Russians some years previous, in regard to schools, marriages, etc. Lithuania wanted all these and other questions solved peaceably by agreement. Even with the leaders of the Protestant denomination Lithuania made an agreement to settle the difficulties which were of interest to the State and the Evangelical Church.[31]

Lithuania also had international motives for making a concordat with the Vatican. After World War I the prestige of the Vatican, the representative of the Moral Power, was high.[32] The new Lithuania was seeking more friends and protectors in international life.[33] Lithuania was eager by international acts and by agreements

[31] The Lithuanian Government together with the Directorium of Klaipėda (Memel) signed, on July 31, 1925, an agreement with *Die Evangelische Kirche der altpreuszischen Union.* By this agreement the Evangelical Church obtained autonomy in Klaipėda and the Lithuanian Government received some concessions regarding the appointments of Church officials. — Cf. C. Boosz, "Katholische Konkordate und evangelische Kirchenverträge unter besonderer Berücksichtigung des ev. Memelabkommens von 1925"—*Archiv für katholisches Kirchenrecht,* CVII (1927), 33-44.

[32] Cf. M. Bierbaum, *Das Konkordat in Kultur. Politik und Recht* (Freiburg im Br.: Herder und Co., 1928), p. 4.

[33] In the name of the Lithuanian Government, on March 24, 1918, a petition was sent to the Nuncio, Archbishop Eugenio Pacelli, in Munich, asking for his intercession that Lithuania be recognized by the Vatican as an independent state: "Die unterzeichnete Delegation bittet durch Vermittlung Euer Exzellenz seiner Heiligkeit das Ersuchen unterbreiten zu dürfen, bereits jetzt Litauen als freien und unabhängigen Stat mit der Hauptstadt Wilna anzuerkennen. Gleichzeitig bittet die unterzeichnete Delegation Seine Heiligkeit, Litauen, dessen katholische Bevölkerung immer mit besonderer Treue dem H. Stuhl angehangen hat, besonders Allerhöchstes Wohlwollen entgegenbringen und den Apostolischen Segen dem ganzen Litauischen Volk und der unterzeichneten Abordnung erteilen zu wollen. Mit dem Ausdruck der ausgezeichneten Hochachtung haben wir die Ehre, zu sein Euer Exzellenz ganz ergebene Dr. J. Šaulys, J. Staugaitis, J. Vileišis." — P. Klimas, *Der Werdegang des Litauischen Staates von 1915 bis zur Bildung der provisorischen Regierung im November 1918* (Berlin: Pasz und Garleb G. m. b. H., 1919), p. 122.

to confirm and to express her sovereignty.[34]

It was a happy day for Lithuanians when, on November 10, 1922, their country was recognized *de iure* by the Holy See.[35] Lithuania, then, was ready for a Concordat. Towards the close of 1922 a concordat was promulgated with Latvia,[36] a neighboring state of Lithuania, and this provided another incentive for Lithuania to conclude an agreement with the Vatican.

[34] "Auch beim Konkordats abschlusz von Litauen handelte es sich um den Abschlusz eines Staates, der infolge der Neugestaltung Europas groszen Wert auf politische Selbständigkeit legte und durch den Abschlusz eines Konkordates mit dem Heiligen Stuhl seine Souveränität zum Ausdruck bringen wollte."—H. Kiszling, *Abschlusz und Inhalt der neueren Konkordate* (Tübingen: E. Göbel, 1931), p. 51.

[35] The Lithuanian Government received the following document from the Vatican: "Segretario di Stato di Sua Santità. Dal Vaticano, 10 Novembre, 1922. "Le soussigné Cardinal Secrétaire d'Etat de Sa Sainteté a le plaisir de vous communiquer que le Saint Siège est heureux de reconnaître *de jure* le Gouvernment de Lithuanie. Il forme les voeux le plus ardents pour la prospérité de la Noble Nation Lithuanienne et souhaite vivement qu'une *aimable entente* puisse avoir lieu au plus tôt entre la Lithuanie et la Pologne, dans la certitude que cet heureux rapprochment contribuera à rendre toujours plus cordiales les relations entre le Saint Siège et les deux noble nations.

Le Cardinal soussigné profite volontiers de l'occasion qui lui est offerte pour Vous réitérer l'homage de sa haute considération. Signé: E. [P.?] Gasparri."—G. Rutenberg, *Die baltischen Staaten und das Völkerrecht* (Riga: Verlag der Buchhandlung G. Loefler. 1928), p. 152.

It can be understood why recognition came comparatively so late, since the Lithuanian Constitution was promulgated only on August 6, 1922; recognition on the part of the Allies of World War I (England, France, Italy and Japan) came even later, December 20, 1922.

[36] It was concluded on May 20, 1922; the exchange of the documents of ratification took place on November 3, 1923.—A. Perugini, *Concordata Vigentia* (Romae: Pontificium Institutum Utriusque Iuris, 1934), pp. 3-8.

Chapter III

AIMS OF THE CHURCH AFTER THE PROMULGATION OF THE CODE AND AFTER WORLD WAR I

1. The Code of Canon Law and the New Era of Concordats

The severe and destructive war did not hinder the Church from finishing the great work of codification, which was started by Pius X and accomplished under the Pontificate of Benedict XV. On May 27, 1917, the new *Codex Iuris Canonici* was promulgated. The aim of the Holy See was to enforce the canons of the new Code throughout the world. However, this was not easy to attain. First of all, the Church in many countries was bound by former agreements, which the new Code left in force;[1] and this was in many cases really inconvenient, because, e.g., in some states the Catholic dynasties, in favor of which a number of important privileges had been given, no longer held power, and had even been replaced by very liberal governments. Secondly, some forms of the Code (e.g., about marriages, schools, and education), to be really effective, postulated a cooperation on the part of the rulers of different countries, by means of their particular legislation.

There arose other special questions in post-war Europe: the territorial changes were enormous and the boundaries of dioceses had to be reorganized; the rights of religious minorities had to be protected; legal support for new Church activities such as Catholic Action had to be obtained. But, on the other hand, the war changed the situation in favor of the Code and the aims of the Catholic Church. The reorganization of Europe was a substantial one. For this reason Benedict XV in his allocution *In hac quidem,* on November 21, 1921, made it clear that some states could no longer be considered to be the same moral entity with

[1] Canon 3: "Codicis canones initas ab Apostolica Sede cum variis Nationibus conventiones nullatenus abrogant aut iis aliquid obrogant; eae idcirco perinde ac in praesens vigere pergent, contrariis huius Codicis praescriptis minime obstantibus."

which the Holy See had formerly treated; and, therefore, these new states had no right to claim privileges which the Holy See by special conventions or concordats had conceded to the states in their former status. The Head of the Church, however, expressed his willingness to conclude new agreements, more adapted to the changed conditions.[2]

The rulers of practically every nation, as Pius XI expressed it,[3] motivated by a desire for union and peace, had turned to the Holy See in order to settle the legal questions of interest to both Church and State. The clear norms of the new Code were of considerable help for finding the proper solution; often the new concordats simply referred to canons of the Code.[4]

The staff of Apostolic Delegates, Nuncios, and Internuncios increased greatly. This helped the Holy See always to be well informed on various situations, and to negotiate new agreements

[2] "Etenim nemo est qui ignoret, post recens immane bellum, vel novas natas esse Respublicas, vel Respublicas veteres, provinciis sibi adiunctis, crevisse. Iam vero, ut alia omitamus quae huc possumus affere, patet quae privilegia pridem haec Apostolica Sedes, per pactiones sollemnes conventionesque, aliis concesserat, eadem nullo iure posse hasce Respublicas sibi vindicare, cum res inter alios acta neque emolumentum neque praeiudicium ceteris afferat. Item Civitates nonnullas videmus ex hac tanta conversione rerum funditus novatas extitisse, adeo ut quae nunc est, non illa ipsa possit haberi moralis, ut aiunt, persona, quacum Apostolica Sedes olim convenerat. Ex quo illud natura consequitur, ut etiam pacta et conventa, quae inter Apostolicam Sedem et eas Civitates antehac intercesserant, vim iam suam omnem omiserint.

Verum si qui Republicis vel Civitatibus quas diximus praepositi sunt, velint cum Ecclesia pacisci concordiam aliis condicionibus quae mutatis temporibus melius congruant, sciant Apostolicam Sedem—nisi quid aliam ob causam sit impedimento-non recusaturam quominus ea de re cum ipsis agat, ut cum aliquot iam agere instituit."*AAS,* XIII (1921), 521-522.

[3] Encyclical *Ubi arcano Dei,* December 23, 1922: " . . . principes plerosque viros ac nationum rectores paene omnium, uno veluti instinctu pacis permotos, cum hac Apostolica Sede seu veterem revocare amicitiam, seu primum pacisci concordiam quasi certatim voluisse."—*AAS,* XIV (1922), 697.

[4] Cf. A. Bertola, "Attività Concordataria e Codificazione del Diritto della Chiesa"—*Archivio Giuridico,* CXI (1934), 174.

which, by their clear recognition of the rights of the Church, could serve as precedents and examples for other countries.[5]

2. The International Activity of Pope Pius XI

The authority and influence of the Holy See after World War I was great. Providence had raised to the See of Peter Pope Pius XI, a man who was internationally minded and who understood the situation.[6]

In the reign of Pius XI history witnesses a new era of concordats.[7] During the first twelve years of the pontificate (1922-1934), His Holiness concluded agreements with as many as thirteen states, including the very important treaty with the Italian Government, solving the well known Roman Question.[8] The agreements

[5] Cf. Yves de la Brière, "La Renaissance Contemporaine du Droit Canonique dans plusiers Législations Séculières Grâce aux divers Concordats du Pontificat de Pie XI"—*Revue de Droit International et de Législation Comparée,* XVI (1935), 217-218.

[6] C. C. Eckhardt, a non-Catholic professor of History in the University of Colorado, in his book *The Papacy and World Affairs* (Chicago: The University of Chicago Press, 1937), pp. 262-263 writes: "Remarkable is the suggestion of a Protestant (Congregational) pastor, the Rev. John M. Phillips, of Hartford, Connecticut, that Christians, of every denomination, and Jews, appeal to Pope Pius XI to lead a world-movement against war, to end war through a religious truce similar to those of medieval times. . . . The significant point is the assertion by a Protestant minister that 'the Pope's position of authority makes him the most distinguished social leader of the day' (*New York Times,* Jan. 29, 1935, p. 6, col. 5)."

[7] "Dopo il grande conflitto mondiale la Santa Sede ha concluso, con una frequenza che ha rarissimi riscontri nel passato . . . numerosi concordati, che presentano particolare interesse, oltre che per i cultori di diritto ecclesiastico, anche per gli studiosi del diritto publico in generale."—G. Lampis, "Il Concordato tra la Santa Sede e lo Stato Lituano"—*Rivista di Diritto Pubblico,* XXI (1929), 227.

[8] Cf. A. Perugini, *Concordata Vigentia,* p. vii; J. Prunskis, "Pijaus XI Konkordatų Politika" (The Policy of the Concordats of Pius XI) in the book *Pijus XI* (Marijampolė: Liet. Moterų Kultūros dr-ja, 1937), pp. 285-305.

were signed with states of very different conditions: large and small, great powers with old traditions and weak states of recent origin.[9] As Pope Pius XI, on June 3, 1933, expressed it in the Encyclical *Dilectissima Nobis,*[10] the Catholic Church is never committed to one form of government in preference to all others. She does not have any difficulty in adapting herself to various civil institutions, and sincere agreements with them are of advantage not only to the Church, but to the State as well.

Pope Pius XI will remain great because of his international activity, and his contribution to positive international law by means of the various concordats established during his reign.[11] Lithuania was not forgotten in his far-reaching undertakings.

[9] Cf. B. Wilanowski, "Stosunek Kosciola do Państwa w Swietle Ostatnich Konkordatów"—*Rocznik Prawniczy Wilenski,* IV (1930), 185.

[10] "Omnibus siquidem in comperto est Catholicam Ecclesiam cum prae aliis nullam rei publicae ordinationem potiorem habeat, dummodo Dei christianaeque conscientiae iura sarta tectaque evadant tum quibusvis civilibus societatibus, ulla non interposita difficultate, convenire; sive eaedem Regni, sive Reipublicae formam induant, sive denique ab optimatium, sive a popularium dominatu pendeant.

Cuius rei argumento sunto, ut recentiora tantummodo attingamus facta, non pauca ea pactiones et "Concordata" quae vocant, postremis etiam hisce temporibus digesta: itemque necessitudinis rationes, quae Apostolicae Sedi cum variis civitatibus intercedunt; cum iis etiam, quae, post proximum maximumque bellum, regio imperio rejecto, in Reipublicae ordinationem coaluerunt.

Iamvero, numquam hae Reipublicae—et ad sua instituta et ad iustae amplitudinis studia et ad gentis suae prosperitatem quod attinet—numquam, dicimus, neque ex susceptis amicitiae officiis cum Apostolica hac Sede, neque ex inito consilio, conventiones scilicet, horum temporum conditioni consentaneas, iis de rebus mutua fide transigendi, quae ad civilem et ad ecclesiasticam societatem pertinent, ulla procul dubio detrimenta ceperunt.

Quin immo, cum de re agatur omnino explorata ac certa, asseverare possumus ex hac fiduciae plena, Ecclesiae Civitatumque concordia, non exigua orta esse civilibus consortibus commoda atque utilitates."—*AAS,* XXV (1939), 262-.63.

[11] S. Goyeneche finishes his study about the effectiveness of the work of Pius XI in the field of law with these words: "Pius XI ob eius

3. The Vatican and Lithuania.

World War I left Lithuania very badly devastated and the Holy See was prompt to supply help. Already on March 13, 1916, that is, two years before Lithuania proclaimed her independence, the Pope sent to the suffering nation a charitable subsidy of ten thousand lire.[12]

One year later, Pope Benedict XV, in his fatherly solicitude, gave his consent for a declaration of Lithuanian Day (to be held on the Sunday within the Octave of the Ascension, which that year fell on May 20, 1917), a day on which, in Catholic churches throughout the world, public prayers were offered for Lithuania and a collection was taken for the poor.[13] Lithuanian Day turned the eyes of the world upon this nation and Catholics responded with generous support.[14]

actuosissimam et variam operositatem legiferam nedum inter primos legum conditores, verum etiam inter magnos iuris canonici fautores esse annumerandum."—"De Pii PP. XI operositate legifera" — *Apollinaris,* XII (1939), 489; cf. N. Hilling, "Die Gesetzgebung des Pius XI" — *Archiv für katholisches Kirchenrecht,* CXIX (1939), 309-351, CXX (1940), 4-32.

[12] Cf. *Principles of Peace,* n. 443.

[13] On February 10, 1917, a letter to Bishop F. Karevičius signed by Card. Gasparri, in the name of Pope Benedict XV, stated: "Era dolorosamento noto al Santo Padre come alle populazioni della Lituania sia toccata, nell'imperversare del conflitto europeo, una sorte fra le più miserande, di guisa che le fiorenti campagne e le ricche città di quella travagliata regione sono oggi ridotte a squallore ed a rovina."—*AAS,* IX (1917), 155-126.

[14] Up to November 3, 1917, the Lithuanian Committee in Switzerland received 1,532,000 francs.—A. Viscont, *La Lithuanie Religieuse,* p. 343.

In the name of the nation, at an important convention, held on September 18-22, 1917, at Vilnius, a motion of gratitude was expressed to Pope Benedict XV: "Vilnae. 22 September 1917. Beatissime Pater, Ex omnibus Lithuaniae finibus diversae conditionis deputati ultra ducentos viros in nostra urbe capitali *Vilnae* in nationalem conventum congregati ad deliberandum de misera nostra conditione tempore belli et de futuro libero statu nostrae regionis constituendo, hac occasione libentissime utimur, ut Vestrae Sanctitati summas gratias agamus pro collecta in toto

In the following year the Vatican appointed Msgr. Achille Ratti, the future Pope Pius XI, as Apostolic Visitor to Poland and Lithuania.[15] Lithuania profoundly appreciated the appointment of a Lithuanian Bishop, Jurgis Matulevičius, to the see of Vilnius.[16]

The Apostolic Visitor, Msgr. Ratti, visited Vilnius. He was a guest in the Lithuanian gymnasium (high school) of that town.[17]

The Lithuanians still remember that the Apostolic Visitor, Msgr. Ratti, before his consecration as a Bishop, made a retreat in the Bielany monastery, close to Vilnius. The retreat master was a Lithuanian Bishop, J. Matulevičius. Archbishop Ratti, on Jan. 29-31, 1920, visited the temporary capital of Lithuania, Kaunas, and was received by the President of the Country.

But since relations between Lithuania and Poland were tense, the Vatican decided to appoint a separate Apostolic Visitor for Lithuania. On Nov. 19, 1921, Father A. Zecchini, S.J., was appointed to that post;[18] later, on October 25, 1922, he was designated as Apostolic Delegate.[19] The Lithuanian Government sent

orbe catholico instituta in gratiam lithuanorum bello oppressorum simulque pro paterna *Vestrae Sanctitatis* cura pacis instituendae inter pugnantes nationes, quam summopere exoptamus et qua composita, nostra jura nationalia nos recuperaturos *Vestra Sanctitate* potenter adjuvante speramus et *Vestrae Sanctitatis* benedictionem Apostolicam nostris laboribus humillime adprecamus. Praeses Conferentiae: Dr. J. Basanavičius." — P. Klimas, *Der Werdegang des litauischen Staates,* p. 64.

[15] *AAS,* X (1918), 227-228.

The reason for sending only one Visitor to both countries was traceable to tradition which dated from the time Poland and Lithuania were united. This tradition was abandoned later when separate Constitutions of Lithuania and of Poland were proclaimed, and when both countries officially changed their intention to remain together.—Cf. P. P. Būčys, "Pijaus XI Darbai Lietuvai"—*Pijus XI,* p. 334.

[16] He was consecrated on Dec. 1, 1918, and installed on Dec. 8, 1918.—*Arkivyskupas Jurgis Matulevičius* (Marijampolė: Marijonų Spaustuvė, 1933), p. 290.

[17] See the statement of the Director of the Lithuanian Gymnasium, Prof. M. Biržiška, in the book *Arkivyskupas Jurgis Matulevičius,* p. 149.

[18] *AAS,* XIII (1821), 549. He was appointed also Apostolic Visitor for Latvia and Estonia.

[19] *AAS,* XIV (1922), 608.

Msgr. Dr. J. Narjauskas to Rome; later, after Lithuania was recognized *de iure,* Minister K. Bizauskas was appointed at the Vatican.[20]

The Foreign Ministry started negotiations about the concordat, but an uprising in Klaipėda (Memel) and the return of that region to Lithuania in 1923 kept the Lithuanian diplomats very busy during that year and the next. It was even found necessary to recall Minister Bizauskas to Lithuania. *Chargé d'affaires* J. Macevičius remained at the Vatican, but not much progress was made in negotiations. However, relations between the Vatican and Lithuania continued to be friendly and sincere.

[20] Elsewhere unpublished material about the relations between the Vatican and Lithuania is given by Bishop P. P. Būčys, "Pijaus XI Darbai Lietuvai"—*Pijus XI,* pp. 333-377. Bishop Būčys, former Rector of the University of Kaunas, was an intimate friend of Archbishop J. Matulevičius, who was Apostolic Visitor in Lithuania; both were founders of the Congregation of Marian Fathers.

Chapter IV

CRITICAL PERIOD IN THE RELATIONS BETWEEN THE HOLY SEE AND LITHUANIA

1. Lithuanian Aspirations towards Vilnius.

A deep historical and national sentiment and the ties of blood bound the Lithuanians to Vilnius and to the people of that region. Vilnius was founded by the Grand Dukes of Lithuania, and the Lithuanian capital was established there.[1]

During the Russian occupation (1795-1914) Vilnius remained at least the cultural and administrative center of Lithuania. The former union with Poland, the fact that Catholicity was introduced into Lithuania by the Polish clergy, and the prohibition of the Lithuanian press by the Russians were reasons why some inhabitants of the Vilnius region (which was closer to Poland than any other part of Lithuania) were influenced, more or less, by the Polish culture. The whole region of Vilnius was divided into districts. According to the census taken in 1897 by the Russian Government, there were in the district of Vilnius 76,000 Lithuanians, and 73,100 who called themselves Poles; in the district of Švenčionys, 58,100 Lithuanians and 10,300 Poles; in the district of Trakai, 118,200 Lithuanians, and 22,900 Poles; in the district of Lida, 17,800 Lithuanians and 9,600 Poles. A large percentage of the population consisted of White Russians.[2]

The first national *Seimas* of Lithuania, known as the Great Lithuanian *Seimas,* was held in Vilnius, and the representatives of the nation demanded autonomy for Lithuania with Vilnius as its capital. Lithuanian Independence was proclaimed on February 16, 1918, in Vilnius, and that city itself was declared the capi-

[1] J. Ehret, *La Lithuanie* (Genève: Edition Altar, 1919), p. 21; A. Šapoka, *Lietuvos Istorija,* pp. 76-93.

[2] *Statistinės Žinios apie Lietuvą ligi Karui 1914 m.* (The Statistical Information on Lithuania before the War of 1914; Kaunas: Prekybos ir Pramonės Ministerija, 1919), pp. 36-37.

tal of Lithuania.[3] The first body of the Government of Lithuania was organized in Vilnius, November 11, 1918.[4]

Russia, in the peace treaty signed at Moscow on July 12, 1920, recognized Independent Lithuania, with the Vilnius region included as part of it.[5] The Lithuanians, however, had to wage war with the Poles for Vilnius. It was a prolonged war in the struggle of the people for independence. Finally, on October 7, 1920, at Suvalkai, an agreement was signed with Poland.[6] According to the agreement, war operations were to cease. A line of demarcation was drawn. It was supposed to remain in force until all Polish-Lithuanian disputes should be peacefully settled. Vilnius was left under Lithuanian control.

But a supposedly mutinous general, Želigowsky, on the day after the signing of the treaty of Suvalkai, attacked the Lithuanian forces, and on October 9, 1920, occupied Vilnius. The Lithuanian Government sent a protest to the League of Nations. The President of the Council of the League, Leon Burgeois, on October 14, 1920, published an energetic protest against the breaking of the international agreement.[7] From that time forward till March 19, 1939, Lithuania did not have official diplomatic relations with Poland.

The occupants of Vilnius started to "polonize" that region. Many Lithuanian schools were closed, a number of Lithuanian organizations were suppressed, and even some of the much-

[3] See photostatic copy of the Act of Independence in S. Šapoka, *Lietuvos Istorija,* p. 544.

[4] "The Vilnius Question,"—*Lithuanian Government Statistical Almanac, 1937* ([Kaunas]: Central Statistic Bureau [1937]), p. 348.

[5] *League of Nations Treaty Series,* III (1921), 122.

[6] *Conflit Polono-Lithuanien.* Question de Vilna. Documents Diplomatique (Kaunas: Ministère des Affaires Étrangères, 1924), pp. 56-58.

[7] "L'occupation de Vilna est donc une violation des engagements pris vis-à-vis du Conseil de la Société des Nations et il est impossible à celui-ci de na pas demander au Gouvernment polonais quelles mesures immédiates il compte prendre pour assurer le respect des engagements."—*Conflit Polono-Lithuanien. Documents Diplomatique,* pp. 93-94.

cherished crosses which the Lithuanians had set up in the fields were removed because they were decorated with Lithuanian colors and ornaments. In addition to all this some Lithuanian patriots were imprisoned, and some also killed.[8] These facts, even apart from any discussion of the essential problems of that region, lead one to understand the aspirations of Lithuanians towards Vilnius and their sentiments towards Poland. Lithuania did not have any diplomatic relations with Poland, and nobody interfered in the absolute freedom of the Lithuanian press to describe these deeds in detail.[9]

2. The Polish Concordat and the Lithuanian Reaction.

The occupational Polish forces organized a body of representatives of the Vilnius region, which on February 20, 1922, decided to incorporate that region as a part of Poland. After this was done, on March 28, 1922, this body of representatives was dismissed.[10] As the maxim says, *melior est conditio possidentis.*[11] And so it was with Vilnius. It remained under Polish rule, and the Conference of Ambassadors on March 15, 1923, assigned the Vilnius region to Poland.[12]

[8] B. Šėmis [M. Biržiška], *Vilniaus Golgota* (Golgotha of Vilnius; Kaunas: Vilniui Vaduoti Sąjunga, 1930).

[9] L. .P M. Le Bideau at the University of Algiers wrote a dissertation for the degree of Doctor of Law: *Les Relations Lithuano-Polonaise* (Université d'Alger, Facultéde Droit, 1934).

See also C. Graužinis, *La Question de Vilna* (Paris: Jouve et Cie., 1927); L. Natkevičius, *Aspect Politique et Juridique du Différend Polono-Lithuanien* (4. ed., Paris: E. Duchemin, 1930).

[10] A. Šapoka, *Lietuvos Istorija,* p. 566.

[11] Cf. Reg. LXV, R. J., in VI°.

[12] "Decision de la Conference des Ambassadeurs, au sujet des Frontiers de la Pologne du 15 Mars 1923"—*Conflit Polono-Lithuanien, Documents Diplomatique,* pp. 376-382. Cf. *Consultations de M. A. de Lapradelle, Louis de Le Fur et André N. Mandelstam concernant la Decision de la Conference des Ambassadeurs du 15 Mars 1923* (Paris: Jouve et Cie., 1928).

The able Polish diplomats now started to work on a concordat. The Vatican, having in mind the solution of the Vilnius question as affected by the Conference of Ambassadors, and seeing the great need to put in order various religious problems in Poland, concluded a concordat with that country. It was signed on February 10, 1925, and the exchange of the documents of ratification occurred on June 2, 1925, in Warsaw.[13]

The Vilnius region, according to article IX of the Polish Concordat, was included in the Polish ecclesiastical province, and some concessions were made to the Polish President of State concerning the appointment of the Archbishop of Vilnius: the Vatican was bound to get in touch with the Polish President of State before the appointment of a Bishop to the See of Vilnius (art. XI), and the Bishop of Vilnius had to take an oath of fidelity to the Polish President of State (art. XII).

After the ratification of this concordat with Poland excitement in Lithuanian ran high.[14] The Lithuanians of Vilnius expressed their protest.[15] In Kaunas, the temporary capital of Lithuania, a mass meeting and demonstration took place before the residence of the Apostolic Delegate. The police suppressed the demonstra-

[13] *AAS,* XVII (1925), 273-287; A. Perugini, *Concordata Vigentia,* pp. 35-50.

[14] Lituani " . . . constatavano che il loro territorio era ecclesiasticamente dipendente tuttora dal metropolita di Varsavia, come ai tempi del dominio zarista."—A. Giannini, *I Concordati Postbellici,* p. 164.

[15] This impressed even jurists of foreign countries. For example, A. Giannini in his book *I Concordati Postbellici,* on p. 152, directly after the text of the Polish Concordat, published an Italian translation of the protest of the Lithuanians of Vilnius, "Dichiarazione del Comitato Provvisorio Lituano di Vilna," in which there is the following statement about the Polish Concordat: "Dandosi la possibilità al Governo civile di intromettersi negli affari ecclesiastici è difficile credere che la conferenza dei Vescovi citata nel paragrafo XXIII del Concordato possa garantire i diritti dei Lituani e degli altri cattolici non polacchi nelle chiese." (p. 154)

Cf. A. Gerstmann, "Na Marginesie Konkordatu"—*Konkordat Polski ze Stolicą Apostolską* (Lwów: Nakładem Tow. "Biblioteka Religijna," 1925), p. 11: " . . . na północy została diecezja Sejneńska przepołowiona, niektóre parafje polskie należały do Kowna, a litewskie do Wilna."

tion, but the Lithuanian government sent a note of protest to the Vatican. The Apostolic Delegate had to leave Lithuania, and the Lithuanian *chargé d'Affaires* at the Vatican, Mr. J. Macevičius, was no longer a *persona grata*. The diplomatic relations between Lithuania and the Vatican were interrupted.[16]

The Bishops of Lithuania in a pastoral letter tried to appease the population by reminding them of the former kindness of the Vatican towards Lithuania,[17] but without considerable success. Many leaders of the Leftist parties used the occasion for propaganda against Catholic groups. In the following election (1926), Christian Democrats and other Catholic parties lost the majority in the *Seimas,* and from that time on they never regained control of the Government.[18] This break between Lithuania and the Vatican left vestiges in their mutual relations which were to remain for a long time.[19]

[16] A. Giannini, *I Concordati Postbellici,* p. 173; N. Turchi, "La Lithuania e il Concordato Polacco"—*L'Europa Orientale,* V (1925), 294.

[17] " . . . sunkiausią mūsų tėvynės valandą, kuomet baisiojo karo metu badas ir vargas labiausiai slėgė visus lietuvius, Šv. Tėvas vienas pakėlė savo balsą už mus, paskelbė visam pasauliui Lietuvos vardą . . . "—Pastoral Letter of the Bishops of Lithuania on March 21, 1925.—*Tiesos Kelias* (Official Organ of the Lithuanian Clergy. Hereinafter cited as *TK*), Official part, I (1925), 23.

[18] Another reason for their failure to regain control of the Government was the lack of any further opportunity, since the elections of 1926 were the last full democratic elections.

[19] Cf. A. Jaščenka, *Tarptautinės Teisės Kursas* (Kaunas: V. D. Universiteto Teisių Skyriaus leidinys, 1931), p. 572: "Lietuvos santykiams su Vatikanu suduotas didelis smūgis, Šventajam Sostui sudarius konkordatą su Lenkija 1925. II. 10."

Chapter V

THE APOSTOLIC CONSTITUTION *LITUANORUM GENTE*

1. Archbishop J. Matulevicius—Apostolic Visitor in Lithuania.

Both the Vatican and the Lithuanian Government, which at that time was in majority Catholic, felt that something had to be done. The Vatican, understanding what feelings the Lithuanians might have towards a diplomat sent from Rome, on December 8, 1925, appointed to the post of Apostolic Visitor a Lithuanian, Archbishop J. Matulevičius, who had resigned as Bishop of Vilnius. He was the former inspector of the Theological Academy in Petersburg; he was one of the supporters of the agrarian reform in Lithuania; and he enjoyed great respect throughout the whole nation.[1] So Archbishop J. Matulevičius became the first Apostolic Visitor appointed exclusively for Lithuania.

The new Apostolic Visitor arrived at Kaunas and approached the Minister of Foreign Affairs, Msgr. M. Reinys (now Archbishop of Vilnius). They both agreed on the following plan of action: first, that there be established an ecclesiastical province in Lithuania; then, that diplomatic relations be resumed with the Vatican; and finally, that a concordat be concluded.[2]

The Apostolic Visitor, having the support of the Lithuanian Government, started to work on establishing an ecclesiastical province in Lithuania. This was an old dream of the country. The first Lithuanian king, Mindaugas (13th century), and the famous Lithuanian Duke, Vytautas the Great (died October 27, 1430), had tried to organize an ecclesiastical province in Lithuania, but did not succeed.[3]

The task now, however, was probably more complicated: the sees and great parts of the two dioceses—Vilnius and Seinai—

[1] P. P. Būčys, "Pijaus XI Darbai Lietuvai"—*Pijus XI*, p. 354.

[2] See the statement of Archbishop M. Reinys, *Arkivyskupas Jurgis Matulevičius*, p. 99.

[3] P. P. Būčys, "Pijaus XI Darbai Lietuvai"—*Pijus XI*, p. 358.

were under foreign rule; Klaipėda was included in the Lithuanian State, but Church affairs in that district, according to the Klaipėda (Memel) Convention of 1924, sect. 5,[4] were to enjoy autonomy. In Klaipėda there were only about 6,000 Catholics, organized into four parishes. It was impossible, therefore, to include them as a deanery in the nearest Lithuanian diocese, but, on the other hand, they were too few in number to warrant the creation of a separate diocese.[5]

Archbishop J. Matulevičius, thanks to the great generosity of Pope Pius XI, was successful in finding ways to solve these complicated problems.

2. The Establishment of an Ecclesiastical Province in Lithuania

Through the centuries the feast of Easter, 1926, will remain a great day for the Lithuanian Church. On that feast, which fell on April 4, an ecclesiastical province was established in Lithuania by the Apostolic Constitution *Lituanorum Gente,* which was promulgated on April 6, 1926.[6]

In this document, His Holiness, Pope Pius XI, lauds the faith and piety of the Lithuanian nation, and states that for the prosperity of the Catholic religion, as well as of the State itself, he is establishing the Ecclesiastical Province of Lithuania, consisting of five dioceses: the metropolitan Kaunas and the suffragan dioceses of Kaišedorys, Panevėžys, Telšiai and Vilkaviškis.[7] The district of Klaipėda, until that time a part of the German Ecclesiastical Province, was now transformed into a *Praelatura nullius*

[4] Pr. Dailydė, *Lietuvos Sutartys su Svetimomis Valstybėmis.* Recueil des Traités Conclus par la Lithuanie avec Le Pays Etrangers, I, 271.

[5] Cf. P. P. Būčys, *op. cit.*, p. 356.

[6] *AAS,* XVIII (1926), 121-123. It was reprinted in *L'Europa Orientale,* VI (1926), 376-378. Original Latin text and the Lithuanian translation were published in Lithuania on April 19, 1926, in the official part of the magazine of the Lithuanian clergy, *TK,* I (1926), 24-28.

[7] "Lituanorum gente post bellum maximum in libertatem, Deo favente, tandem restituta, Nos, qui eorum fidem ac pietatem, tam strenue diuque in adversis rebus omne genus servatas, praesentes conspicati sumus, cum persuasum habeamus aptiorem ecclesiasticarum rerum dispositionem plurimum sane conferre, non modo ad catholici nominis incrementum, sed

under the jurisdiction of Bishop J. Staugaitis, who was also the Ordinary of Telšiai. Moreover, the Apostolic Constitution *Lituanorum Gente* reserved to the Pope the power to make any necessary changes in the future.[8] All priests actually having an assignment within the territory of any of these new dioceses were *ipso facto* incardinated into the service of that diocese. All documents were ordered to be sent to the dioceses where they belonged by virtue of the new Apostolic Constitution.

By the Apostolic Constitution *Lituanorum Gente* there were formed 5 dioceses, 50 deaneries (the *Praelatura nullius* included) and about 500 parishes.[9] The Holy See appointed the new Bishops for Lithuania.[10] The Apostolic See by establishing an ecclesias-

etiam ad ipsam rei civilis prosperitatem apprime utile atque opportunum existimamus ut in Lituania dioeceses et numero augeantur et in provinciam ecclesiasticam constituantur.

Nos igitur, quibus incumbit, pro Apostolico munere dioecesium fines statuere, de Apostolicae potestatis plenitudine ac certa scientia, suppleto quorum interest vel interesse praesumant consensu, decernimus ut ex omnibus illis territoriis, quae modo in finibus Lituaniae Reipublicae sita sunt, propria constituatur Provincia Ecclesiastica, quaeque constabit: sede Kaunensi, uti metropolitana, et dioecesibus: Telšensi una cum Praelatura Klaipedensi, Panevežensi, Vilkaviškensi et Kaišedorensi, uti suffraganeis."—*AAS,* XVIII (1926), 121.

The large diocese of Samogitia was divided into three dioceses: the Metropolitan Archdiocese of Kaunas and the suffragan dioceses of Panevėžys and Telšiai. The largest part of the dioceses of Vilnius and Seinai were under Polish occupation; from the parts united with Lithuania were formed the suffragan dioceses of Kaišedorys and of Vilkaviškis.

Large parts of some regions were under foreign domination. To avoid any complication the new dioceses were named, not according to the names of the regions, but according to the names of the principal city of the section in which the See of the Bishop was erected.

[8] "Reservamus tamen Nobis Sedique Apostolicae facultatem dictas circumscriptiones, pro temporum adiunctis, quoties opportunum in Domino visum fuerit, modificandi, immutandi et aliter definiendi."—*AAS,* XVIII (1926), 123.

[9] The map of the Lithuanian Ecclesiastical Province is printed in *JP,* IX (1929), 275.

[10] His Excellency, P. Karevičius, Ordinary of the diocese of Samogita,

tical province showed, as it was expressed by Archbishop J. Matulevičius in his letter to the Minister of Foreign Affairs, a profound understanding of the needs of Lithuania and evidenced its own great generosity.[11]

The liberation of the Lithuanian dioceses from subjection to foreign Metropolitan Sees was considered by Lithuanians and by others as equivalent to the gaining of freedom in matters of religion, and as the completion of the independence of the country.[12]

resigned. In his place Archbishop J. Skvireckas was appointed to the new Metropolitan See of Kaunas. The Bishop of the diocese of Seinai, A. Karosas, was transferred to the newly formed diocese of Vilkaviškis, but because of his advanced years the Holy See appointed to the See of Vilkaviškis Bishop M. Reinys as coadjutor with the right of succession. To the diocese of Telšiai was appointed Bishop J. Staugaitis; to the diocese of Kaišedorys, Bishop J. Kukta; and to the diocese of Panevėžys, Bishop A. Paltarokas.—*AAS,* XVIII (1926), 132.

[11] "Apaštalų Sostas, taip greitai ir taip svarbius reikalus ir dar tokia gražia forma atlikdamas Lietuvos Bažnyčios ir Tautos naudai, parodė tikro atjautimo Lietuvos reikalų ir norėjo išreikšti Lietuvai ypatingo palankumo."—*Arkivyskupas Jurgis Matulevičius,* p. 100.

[12] "Popiežiaus Pijaus XI pirmaeilės istorinės reikšmės darbas, bažnytinės provincijos sudarymas, užbaigė nepriklausomos Lietuvos kūrimo darbą, nes mūsų valstybę padarė dvasinėje srityje pilnai sutvarkytą. Jei šis didysis Popiežius tik tą vieną darbą būtų Lietuvai padaręs, jo vardas turėtų likti amžinai aukso raidėmis išrašytas mūsų istorijoje." — P. P. Būčys, "Pijaus XI Darbai Lietuvai"— *Pijus XI,* p. 358.

Cf. R. Ruzé, "A propos des Nouveaux Accords du Saint-Siège"—*Revue de Droit International et de Législation Comparée,* X (1929), 342: "Rome assurait l'indépendence religieux du nouvel Etat vis-a-vis de ses voisins par la création d'un archevêché sur son territoire qui ne contenait alors que des évêchés."

A. Giannini, "La Costituzione Apostolica *Lituanorum Gente*"—*L'Europa Orientale,* VI (1926), 375: "Acceno che riuscì particolarmente caro ai cattolici lituani, i quali videro nella costituzione apostolica non solo coronato il desiderio di una gerarchia ecclesiastica nazionale, numericamente adequata ai loro bisogni, ma anche il riconoscimento, da parte del Vicario di Christo, dell'ardore e della tenacia con cui seppero resistere nei duri tempi della schiavitù alla minaccia dilagante ed opprimente dell'aggressiva chiesa ortodossa."

Chapter VI

THE FRAMING OF THE LITHUANIAN CONCORDAT

1. The Negotiations and the Signing of the Agreement

The negotiations with the Vatican for a concordat were initiated in 1923, the year after Lithuania was recognized *de iure* by the Holy See.[1]

Discussion of the principles of the new agreement, however, made no considerable progress; the Lithuanian Government was too busy with the reconstruction of the internal life of the new state, and with such essential and strictly temporal affairs as the problems of the unique port of Lithuania, the city and district of Klaipėda. The Vatican was satisfied inasmuch as the Catholic Government of Lithuania already of its own accord respected the freedom of religion and the rights of the Church. However, the sudden interruption of diplomatic relations between the Vatican and Lithuania after the Polish Concordat resulted in a suspension of negotiations for a similar concordat with Lithuania.

The Left-wing Government came to power in Lithuania during the period June 4-14, 1926.[2] At the end of 1926 the negotiations with the Apostolic Visitor were resumed by the Minister of the Interior, Požela. He had the authorization of the Lithuanian Government, but now the differences in point of view were very considerable. The Leftist Government was planning to establish civil marriage and to grant the right of divorce. Furthermore, it was not particularly inclined to show respect for the Holy See itself.

The resignation of the Leftist Government, as a result of an internal uprising, gradually brought the Nationalists to power. Being in the minority and knowing the majority of the nation to be Catholic, the Nationalists were interested in winning the confidence of the people and in appeasing the Lithuanian clergy by

[1] P. P. Būčys, "Pijaus XI Darbai Lietuvai"—*Pijus XI,* p. 349.

[2] E. J. Harrison, *Lithuania,* p. 214.

concluding the concordat.[3] The new government naturally had a number of issues to resolve, important questions of interest to both Church and State.

The Prime Minister, A. Voldemaras, who was also the Minister of Foreign Affairs, initiated the negotiations with the Apostolic Visitor, Archbishop J. Matulevičius. It took approximately one month to elaborate the basic principles, and on January 17, 1927,[4] the Apostolic Visitor delivered the initial draft of the Concordat to the Minister Voldemaras. The Minister accepted it as a basis for final negotiations. However, the Apostolic Visitor, Archbishop J. Matulevičius died suddenly on January 27, 1927.[5]

Later, on March 10, 1927,[6] in replacing the Apostolic Visitor, the Vatican appointed as the first Internuncio in Lithuania Archbishop Lorenzo Schioppa. This was a sign that relations between the Vatican and Lithuania were indeed becoming much more favorable. During the summer of 1927 the Prime Minister, Professor A. Valdemaras, went to Rome, where already since June 22, 1927, a Lithuanian Minister to the Holy See, Dr. J. Šaulys, had been appointed.[7]

The Prime Minister was anxious to conclude the concordat as

[3] As Yves de la Brière ("La Renaissance Contemporaine du Droit Canonique"—*Revue de Droit International et de Législation Comparée*, XVI [1935], 216) says: " . . . c'était le Saint Siège de Rome, et lui seul, qui était qualifié pour négocier utilement avec les autorités publiques et, en cas de contestation, pour accepter par le clergé et les fidèles les solutions reconnues décentes et opportunes. Que la communauté catholique de tel ou tel Etat fût proportionellement plus ou moins considérable, c'était toujours au Vatican que se trouvait pour elle la clef de la paix religieuse et, pour le gouvernement du pays, la clef de la pacification civile et politique, en tant que connexe avec le problème confessionnel."

[4] The date is not exactly certain, though most probable.—Cf. P. P. Būčys, "Pijaus XI Darbai Lietuvai"—*Pijus XI*, p. 361.

[5] The cause of his death was a complicated case of appendicitis.—I. Česaitis, "Paskutinės Valandos" (The Last Hours)—*Arkivyskupas Jurgis Matulevičius*, p. 49.

[6] *AAS*, XIX (1927), 164.

[7] P. P. Būčys, "Pijaus XI Darbai Lietuvai"—*Pijus XI*, p. 363.

soon as possible. To shorten negotiations he agreed to sign a concordat based on the same principles as the Polish Concordat. However, a number of changes, mostly in favor of the Church, were introduced. For example, there were newly introduced or changed clauses concerning Catholic Action,[8] the military service of the clergy,[9] the provincials of Religious Orders,[10] the keeping of the records of baptisms, of marriages and of deaths,[11] and the status of juridical persons.[12] The Polish Concordat likewise incorporates more restrictions on the property of the Church.[13]

The Lithuanian Concordat does not reproduce art. XX of the Polish Concordat concerning accusations against the clergy because of their political activities, nor art. XXII concerning the rights reserved to the Conference of Bishops to change the language used in Church services or in Church institutions. There are some other less important changes; however, many articles of the Lithuanian Concordat are taken almost *verbatim* from the Polish Concordat.[14]

The Lithuanian Concordat was signed by Cardinal Gasparri

[8] Art. XXV of the Lithuanian Concordat.

[9] Cf. art. V of the Polish and art. V of the Lithuanian Concordat.

[10] See art. X of the Polish and art. X of the Lithuanian Concordat.

[11] Art. XIV of the Lithuanian Concordat.

[12] Cf. art. XVI of the Polish and art. XVII of the Lithuanian Concordat.

[13] Art. XIV and XXIV of the Polish Concordat.

[14] Cf. articles II, III, VI, XI, XII, XVI, XIX, XX, XXVI of the Lithuanian Concordat and articles II, III, VI, XI. XII, XV, XXI, XXII, XXV of the Polish Concordat.

A. Giannini (*I Concordati Postbellici,* p. 222) states: "Si può infatti affermare che le modificazioni ed aggiunte apportate al concordato lituano rispetto a quello polacco si riducono ad ulteriori vantaggi a favore della Chiesa cattolica."

[15] Upon different occasions the signing took place in the capital of the nation party to the concordat: the agreement with France was signed on December 4, 1926, in Paris, while the Concordat with Prussia was signed on June 14, 1929, in Berlin.

and by Prime Minister Voldemaras in Rome [15] on September 27, 1927.[16]

2. The Formal Part of the Lithuanian Concordat.

The Lithuanian Concordat was concluded in the form of a bilateral treaty. It was ratified by the President of State on October 20, 1927.[17] The Holy See ratified the Concordat on December 8,

[16] The first negotiations of the Vatican had been with the democratic governments of Lithuania, but the circumstances then were unfavorable to the making of agreements. As a result, the Concordat was signed with Lithuania at a time when it was represented by the Nationalistic Government. The Vatican, being a spiritual power, abstains from mixing in purely political, internal questions and deals with the government actually representing the country.

Confirmation of this principle can be seen in many official documents of the Holy See. In the letter *Celeberrima evenisse solemnia,* on December 18, 1919, Pope Benedict XV declared that the Church has always been accustomed to be on friendly terms with States, whatever be their constitution.—*AAS,* XII (1920), 33. Pope Pius XI in the Encyclical *Dilectissima Nobis,* on June 3, 1933, stated that "the Catholic Church is never bound to one form of government more than to another . . . She does not find any difficulty in adapting herself to various civil institutions, be they monarchic or republican, aristocratic or democratic."—*AAS,* XXV (1933), 262. Translation from *Encyclical on Spain* (American Press pamphlet). Cf. *Principles of Peace,* n. 1112.

The Church, as any other international power, must sometimes deal even with a *de facto* government. The Catholic statesman and great democrat, Don Luigi Sturzo, in his book *Politics and Morality* (translated by B. Barclay Carter [London: Burns, Oates and Washbourne, 1938], p. 201) said: "The *de facto* government, even if established by a revolution or *coup d'état* or both together. is always regarded by the Church as one that by restoring order, or at least by fixing power in responsible hands, can bring back calm, order, and peace to the country."

[17] E. J. Harrison, *Lithuania,* 215.

The Lithuanian Constitution of 1922, which was in force when the Concordat was signed, requires (sec. 30) confirmation by the *Seimas* for such agreements and treaties which "wholly or partially abolish or amend existing laws, and for agreements which impose duties on Lithuanian citizens."

1927; the exchange of the documents of ratification was made on December 10, 1927, at the Vatican.[18]

The text of the Concordat was promulgated in *Acta Apostolicae Sedis* on December 10, 1927.[19] The Lithuanian Government promulgated it as Law on December 20, 1927.[20] According to art. XXVIII, the Concordat went into effect on the date of the exchange of the documents of ratification, December 10, 1927.

The original text is not in the official Church language, Latin, but in the official diplomatic language, French.[21]

There are norms in the Lithuanian Concordat (cf. art. IV, XXVI) which, in accord with sect. 30 of the Lithuanian Constitution, require that the Concordat be approved by the *Seimas.* The *Seimas,* however, was dissolved on April 12, 1927 and the new elections were delayed. It was for this reason that the President of State himself, as a man in whom executive authority was vested (sect. 40 of the Constitution) and consequently as one who represented the Republic (sec. 46), ratified the Concordat.

18 In the case of the Polish Concordat the exchange of the documents of ratification took place in Warsaw; in the case of the Austrian pact it was at Vienna.

19 *AAS,* XIX (1927), 425-433.

20 *VŽ,* No. 264 (1927), 1-6.

21 At times, in concordats, the language of the nation is used, e. g., the agreements with Italy in 1929 were in the Italian language, and the concordat with Germany (1933) is in both Italian and German, as is the Austrian concordat (1934).

The text of the Lithuanian Concordat is published in various languages. FRENCH: *AAS,* XIX (1927), 425-433; *VŽ,* No. 264 (1927), 1-6; *Apollinaris,* I (1928), 2-7; *Periodica de Re Canonica, Morali, Liturgica,* XVIII (1929), 84-97; *L'Europe Nouvelle,* X (1928), 122-125; *Commentarium pro Religiosis* (Cited hereafter as*CpR*), VIII (1927), 432-439; Pr. Dailydė, *Lietuvos Sutartys su Svetimomis Valstybėmis. Recueil de Traités conclus par la Lithuanie avec le Pays Etrangers,* I, 478-486; A. Perugini, *Concordata vigentia,* pp. 59-70; P. Malakauskis, *Viešosios Bažnytinės Teisės* (The Public Law of the Church, Kaunas: V. D. Universiteto Teologijos-Filosofijos Fakulteto leidinys, 1931), pp. 140-152; *Archiv für katholisches Kirchenrecht,* XVIII (1928), 173-180.

LATIN: *Periodica de Re Morali, Canonica, Liturgica,* XVIII (1929), 84-97.

The Lithuanian. Concordat contains twenty-eight articles, but no additional protocol. The first words of the Concordat are: "In the name of the Most Blessed and Indivisible Trinity." Such is the customary manner in which the Holy See begins a treaty with a Catholic state.[22] This coincided perfectly with the Lithuanian Consitution of that time; it had for its first words: "In the name of Almighty God. . . ."[23]

Further, in the preamble of the Concordat the purpose of the treaty is expressed and the Plenipotentiaries are appointed:

> His Holiness, Pope Pius XI, and the President of the Republic of Lithuania, Mr. Antanas Smetona,
>
> Animated by the desire to determine the situation of the Catholic Church in Lithuania and to establish rules that will govern, in a worthy and stable manner, the ecclesiastical affairs within the territory of the Republic,
>
> Have, for these reasons, decided to conclude a Concordat.
>
> Therefore, His Holiness, Pope Pius XI, and the President of the Republic of Lithuania, Mr. Antanas Smetona, have named their respective Plenipotentiaries,

ENGLISH: A. G. Cicognani, *Canon Law,* authorized English version, by J. M .O'Hara and F. Brennan (2. revised edition, Philadelphia: The Dolphin Press, 1935), pp. 472-474. Here is given the translation only of the most important articles. This translation will be used in the present study. Parts translated by the author of the dissertation will be indicated. An English résumé of the Concordat is given in *The Tablet,* No. 4572 (1927), 865-866.

SPANISH: J. Torrubiano Ripoll, *Los Concordatos de la Postguerra y la Constitucion Religiosa de los Estados* (Madrid: M. Aguilar, 1931), pp. 90-100.

LITHUANIAN: *VŽ,* No. 264 (1927). 1-6; *TK* (official part). IV (1928), 1-12; P. Malakauskis, *Viešosios Bažnytinės Teisės,* pp. 140-152; *Konkordatas tarp Šventojo Sosto ir Lietuvos Valdžios* (Chicago: "Draugas," 1928), 1-16.

[22] Cf. Ottaviani, "Concordatum Lithuanicum"—*Apolinaris,* I (1928), 55.

[23] These first words of the Concordat are a reminder of the obligation of fidelity to the norms of the agreement, because, to use the expression of Abraham Lincoln in his First Inaugural Address. referring to his oath, it is "registered in heaven."—*Speeches and Addresses of Abraham Lincoln* (New York: R. K. Haas, Inc.), p. 23.

His Holiness:

His Eminence Peter Cardinal Gasparri, Secretary of State;

The President of the Republic:

His Excellency, Professor Augustinas Voldemaras, President of the Council and Minister of Foreign Affairs.

The above-mentioned Plenipotentiaries, after the exchange of their credentials, have determined on the following dispositions.

THE CONCLUSION OF THE HISTORICAL SURVEY

How the Lithuanian Concordat was accepted.

The leaders of the Lithuanian Leftist parties had their own objections against such an agreement with the Head of the Roman Catholic Church.[24] Some of members of the Christian Democracy voiced an objection against the similarity of the Lithuanian Concordat with the Polish Concordat, and some politically inclined members of the Lithuanian clergy showed dissatisfaction, because they thought that the Concordat subjected the clergy excessively to the control of the civil administration.[25] Generally, however, there was great satisfaction in Lithuania. The Lithuanian Bishops, in their common pastoral letter, manifested their appreciation of the Concordat, seeing it as an "unusual favor of the Holy See." [26]

The central organization of the Catholic Action movement in Lithuania, *Katalikų Veikimo Centras,* declared in its official cir-

[24] Later, during the years just before World War II, from 1937 on, sincere co-operation between the leaders of Leftist and Catholic groups in Lithuania was established. Both groups, working together against the totalitarian tendencies in the state, and in earnest defense of the democracy and liberty of Lithuania, respected each other's principles.

[25] P. P. Būčys, "Pijaus XI Darbai Lietuvai"—*Pijus XI,* p. 365.

[26] "Šit vėl susilaukėme nepaprastos malonės iš Apaštalų Sosto. Jo Šventenybė Pijus XI aštuntą gruodžio teikėsi patvirtinti nesenai sudarytą Konkordatą tarp Apaštalų Sosto ir Lietuvos Respublikos."—*TK* (offic. part), IV (1928), 13.

cular that the Concordat was the "greatest and most beneficial act of our nation during the year 1927."[27]

The Lithuanian Concordat won great praise even in foreign countries. It was stated that the Concordat expresses great respect for the rights of the Church,[28] and that it is more excellent and more complete than those with Latvia, Bavaria, Poland and France.[29] Finally, even the Lithuanian Constitution was praised for admitting the rights of religion and of the Church.[30]

[27] "Didžiausias ir naudingiausias pereitų metų mūs tautos gyvenimo įvykis buvo sudarymas konkordato su Apaštalų Sostu."—*TK,* IV (1928), 106.

[28] "Jamais le Saint-Siège n'avait encore obtenu d'un gouvernement des stipulations aussi favorable à sa conception des rapports entre spirituel et temporel."—*L'Europe Nouvelle,* X (1928), 117.

[29] Ottaviani, "Concordatum Lithuanicum"—*Apollinaris,* I (1928), 53: "Sollemnis Conventio cum Lithuania . . . nobis videtur inter quattuor praedictas excellentior tum amplitudine et gravitate negotiorum de quibus conventum est, tum etiam opportuna formatione articulorum, quorum maximam partem informant nec pauca nec levia principia iuris publici ecclesiastici."

[30] "È evidente che, dati gli accennati ordinamenti costituzionali, non fosse difficile alla Santa Sede di concludere con la Lituania un concordato assai largo e assai riguardoso degli ordinamenti e delle tradizioni della Chiesa Cattolica. tanto più che il clero lituano si è acquistato larghe benemerenze nella lotta per l'indipendenza e la libertà della Patria."—A. Giannini, *I Concordati Postbellici,* p. 210.

A dissertation about the Lithuanian Concordat was published in Germany: Leo Maser, *Das Konkordat zwischen dem Apostolischen Stuhle und der Republik Litauen vom 27 September 1927 in rechtvergleichender Betrachtung* (Lippstadt in Westfalen: C. J. Laumann, 1931). The study has just 39 pages, and many of them are devoted to the study of the general principles underlying the law of concordats. The author manifests quite plainly a lack of information about conditions in Lithuania and about the juridical life of that country. An example of this is found when he speaks of article XIV of the Concordat, regarding the registering of births, deaths, and marriages. He maintains that this concession was made to the Church because apart from the clergy there were not enough educated Lithuanians to take care of these important records. According to Maser (page 25) almost the only erudite man in Lithuania was Professor A. Valdemaras.

PART TWO

A COMPARATIVE STUDY OF THE LITHUANIAN CONCORDAT

CHAPTER VII

THE GENERAL CONDITION OF THE CHURCH IN LITHUANIA.

1. THE UNION OF CHURCH AND STATE.

The legal structure of the new Lithuania was framed by the Constituent Assembly. In the Constituent Assembly and in the two subsequent *Seimas,* the great majority of the representatives of the nation had sincere respect for religion and for the Church.[1] The *Seimas* had the power to control the Government.[2] Consequently a favorable attitude towards religion and the Church predominated in the Government as well as in the *Seimas* (parliament) of the nation. Both the highest bodies of the legislative and executive power co-operated in building up the union between Church and State in public life.

The historical and legal traditions helped considerably:

1. During the glorious past of Lithuania, from the fourteenth to the sixteenth century, there was an intimate union between the Church and the State.[3] The Catholic Church was one of the greatest factors in the cultural life of the nation, especially during the prolonged occupation of Lithuania by the Russians (1795-1915),[4]

[1] For the composition of the *Seimas* of Lithuania see O. Norem, *Timeless Lithuania,* p. 117. In this same book. p. 115, he writes: "The Christian Democrat party was the strongest numerically and had a firm following amongst the people."

[2] Section 4 and section 59 of the Lithuanian Constitution of 1922.

[3] The Grand Dukes were proponents of religious truths to the people and great supporters of the Church.—A. Šapoka, *Lietuvos Istorija,* p. 136.

[4] As an example, a remarkable system of private schools was developed in Lithuania. In 1804 the Russian administration closed, in the diocese

and merited high recognition in the public life of the country.

2. Lithuania inherited the Russian legal system and also many of its traditions. In Russia, however, the Church of the majority of the people was very closely united with the State.[5] Inherited traditions and laws, along with the fact that the great majority of the people were Catholics, were the main factors that led the Lithuanian State to begin its Constitution with the words: "In the name of Almighty God,"[6] to introduce compulsory religious instruction even in the public schools,[7] and to leave to the Church the offices of performing marriages and of keeping the records of births and of deaths.[8] The State remained in union with the Church.

The new Lithuania recognized the equal rights of all religious organizations existing in the country;[9] Catholicism, however, enjoyed special respect as the religion of the majority.[10] The union

of Samogitia alone, 150 parish schools.—A. Šapoka, *Lietuvos Istorija,* p. 482.

The Catholic Church was a most powerful factor of resistance against the injustices of this Russian administration. Many historical facts on this subject are given in J. Tumas, *Vyskupas Motiejus Valančius. Pastabos Pačiam Sau* (Memoirs of Bishop Valančius; Kaunas: Švietimo Ministerija, 1929) and in A. Alekna. *Katalikų Bažnyčia Lietuvoje,* redagavo J. Stakauskas (The History of the Catholic Church in Lithuania; Kaunas: Šv. Kazimiero Draugija, 1936).

[5] The Czar was the head of the Orthodox Church.—*Сводъ Законовъ Ресійской Имперій,* томъ I, часть I: *Сводъ Основныхъ Государственныхъ Законовъ.* Изданіе 1906 года, ст. 62-66.

[6] Constitution of 1922.

[7] Section 80 of the Constitution of 1922; section 81 of the Constitution of 1928; section 41 of the Constitution of 1938.

[8] Section 85 of the Constitution of 1922; section 86 of the Constitution of 1928 and the later practice.

[9] Section 83 of the Constitution of 1922; section 84 of the Constitution of 1928; cf. sections 27-33 of the Constitution of 1938.

[10] For example, nearly all holidays of the Catholic Church were observed by state institutions; also, at times, the President of the nation, along with the cabinet ministers, assisted at religious celebrations, such as the procession on Corpus Christi.

between State and Church persisted while Lithuania enjoyed her freedom.[11]

The principle of union between the Church and a Catholic state is the teaching of the Holy See. Pope Pius IX condemned the proposition that the state should be separated from the Church.[12]

Leo XIII in the Encyclical *Immortale Dei,* November 1, 1885, declared [13] that according to the natural law and the will of God, Church and State should cooperate. Pius X in the Encyclical *Vehementer No:,* February 11, 1906,[14] and Benedict XV in the Encyclical *Ad Beatissimi,* November 1, 1914,[15] expressed clearly

[11] On August 25, 1940, the Bolsheviks proclaimed the separation of Church and State in Lithuania. Section 96 of "the Constitution of Soviet Lithuania" states: "Piliečių sąžinės laisvei užtikrinti Lietuvos TSR-oje bažnyčia atskirta nuo valstybės ir mokykla nuo bažnyčios. Religinių kultų atlikimo laisvė ir antireliginės propagandos laisvė pripažįstama visiems piliečiáms."—*VŽ,* No. 730 (1940), 662.
It is very significant that this section of the "Soviet Socialistic Lithuanian Constitution" is an exact word for word copy of the Constitution of the Union of Soviet Republics, section 124.—Cf. *Constitutional Provisions Concerning Social and Economic Policy* (Montreal: International Labour Office, 1944), p. 178 and 190.

The Bolsheviks are invaders in Lithuania and their laws are not recognized either by the Vatican or by the representatives of free Lithuania.

[12] Syllabus errorum, prop. 55: "Ecclesia a statu statusque ab Ecclesia seiungendus est."—*ASS,* III (1867), 174; H. Denzinger, *Enchiridion Symbolorum,* n. 1755.

[13] "In negotiis autem mixti iuris. maxime esse secundum naturam itemque secundum Dei consilia non secessionem alterius potestatis ab altera, multoque minus contentionem, sed plane concordiam, eamque cum causis proximis congruentem, quae causae utramque societatem genuerunt."—*ASS,* XVIII (1885, 174; *Codicis Iuris Canonici Fontes cura Emi Petri Card. Gaspari editi* (9 vols., Romae [postea Civitate Vaticana]: Typis Polyglottis Vaticanis, 1923-1939. [Vols. VII-IX ed. cura et studio Emi Iustiniani Card. Serédi], n. 592, § 17. (Hereafter this work is referred to as *Fontes.*)

[14] "Civitatis rationes a rationibus Ecclesiae segregari oportere. profecto falsissima, maximeque perniciosa sententia est."—*ASS,* XXXIX (1906), 5; *Fontes,* n. 671, § 2.

[15] "Meminerint hoc principes rectoresque populorum, ac videant num prudens ac salutare consilium cum potestati publicae tum civitatibus sit

the principle that in the life of the state religion must have its proper place; he declared that the Holy See recommends union between Church and State.

2. The Right of the Church to Pursue her End according to Divine Rules and Canon Law.

The union between Church and State in Lithuania led to ample recognition of the autonomy of the Catholic Church in that country. This is expressed in the first article of the Concordat:

> The Catholic Church, without distinction of rite, shall enjoy in the Republic of Lithuania all the liberties requisite for the exercise of her spiritual powers and jurisdiction, and for the proper conduct and administration of her affairs and property, in conformity with the Divine Law and Sacred Canons.[16]

In the above quoted article, the State explicitly admits the necessary liberties of the Church of the Roman or of the Oriental rite;[17] acknowledges the jurisdictional and administrative power of the Church; and recognizes her right to follow the Divine Law, natural and positive, and the rules of Canon Law.

This recognition of the right of the Church to function according to the Sacred Canons includes the recognition of the general

a sancta Iesu Christi religione discedere, a qua tantum ipsa potestas habet roboris et firmamenti. Etiam atque etiam considerent, num doctrinam Evangelii et Ecclesiae velle a disciplina civitatis, a publica iuventutis institutione exclusam, civilis sapientiae sit. Nimis experiendo cognitum est, ibi hominum iacere auctoritatem, unde exulet religio."—*AAS*, VI (1914), 571; *Fontes*, n. 702, § 9.

[16] "L'Eglise Catholique, sans distinction de Rites, jouira dans la République de Lithuanie de toutes les libertés necessaires à l'exercice de Son pouvoir spirituel et de Sa juridiction ecclésiastique, ainsi qu'a l'administration et gestion de Ses affaires et de Ses biens, conformément aux Lois divines at au Droit Canon."—*AAS*, XIX (1927), 426; A. Perugini, *Concordata vigentia*, p. 59.

[17] There were some Catholics of the Oriental Rite in Lithuania.—Cf. Cappello, "De Natura Concordatorum"—*JP*, VIII (1928), 15.

Bishop P. P. Būčys, a Lithuanian, was consecrated in the Oriental Rite, and is now working in the Congregation for the Oriental Church, in Rome.

and particular laws of the Holy See, of the ordinaries, of ecclesiastical councils and synods, and of all other sources of legislation recognized by Canon Law.[18] The first article of the Concordat harmonizes with the doctrine[19] and the juridical norms of the Church as expressed in canons 100 § 1;[20] 1322, § 2;[21] and 196.[22]

The present Lithuanian Constitution (of 1938) is favorable to the Church as can be seen in the general statements concerning religious organizations:

> Section 27: In its respect for the religious beliefs of its citizens the State shall recognize the Churches and other confessional organizations at present existing in Lithuania.
>
> Section 28. The Churches and other confessional organizations which are recognized by the State shall be allowed freely to impart their beliefs, hold services, maintain their places of worship, and own institutions designated to train subjects for ecclesiastical duties.[23]

[18] Cf. P. Malakauskis, *Viešosios Bažnytinės Teisės,* p. 153.

[19] Cf. Syllabus errorum, prop. 19: "Ecclesia non est vera perfectaque societas plane libera, nec pollet suis propriis et constantibus iuribus sibi a divino suo Redemptore collatis, sed civilis potestatis est difinire quae sint Ecclesiae iura ac limites, intra quos eadem iura exercere queat."—*ASS,* III (1867), 170; H. Denzinger, *Enchiridion Symbolorum,* n. 1719.

[20] "Catholica Ecclesia et Apostolica Sedes moralis personae rationem habent ex ipsa ordinatione divina. . . . "

[21] "Ecclesiae, independenter a qualibet civili potestate, ius est et officium gentes omnes evangelicam doctrinam docendi: hanc vero rite ediscere veramque Ecclesiam amplecti omnes divina lege tenentur."

[22] "Potestas iurisdictionis seu regiminis . . . ex divina institutione est in Ecclesia. . . . "

Cf. also can. 1352; 1496; 1553.

[23] "27 str. Vertindama religiją žmogaus gyvenime, Valstybė pripažįsta esamas Lietuvoje bažnyčias bei kitas tolygias tikybines organizacijas.

28 str. Valstybės pripažintos bažnyčios bei kitos tolygios tikybinės organizacijos gali laisvai skelbti savo mokslą, atlikti savo apeigas, turėti maldų namus ir laikyti dvasines mokyklas dvasininkams ruošti."—*VŽ.* No. 608 (1938), 238.

The writer is in possession of a translation of the Lithuanian Constitution of 1938. The translation was made by officials of the Lithuanian Gen-

Furthermore, section 33 declares:

> The status of churches and other confessional organizations in the State shall be fixed by agreement or by statute.[24]

The Constitution, accepting the principle of agreement between Church and State, endorses the Concordat, and consequently also the right of the Church to pursue her end according to Divine and Canon Law, as expressed in the first article. The general recognition of Divine law and Canon law in the affairs of the Church constitutes them as sources supplementary to the norms expressed in the Lithuanian Concordat, and suggests the direction of its interpretation.

Respecting the freedom of the Church, the State protects the religious freedom of individuals, as is stated in section 20 of Lithuanian Constitution:

> The State shall guard the citizens' freedom of conscience. . . . If they are in the employ of any person, members of all religious denominations shall be granted the time required for the performance of their religious duties.[25]
>
> The state, however warns against all unlawful use of this freedom:
>
> Section 32. The teaching of religious dogmas, the performance of ceremonies and acts of worship, and the other religious activities of the churches and other confessional organizations recognized by the State, as well as their places of worship, shall not be used for a purpose at variance with the Constitution and the laws of the State.
>
> Section 20. . . . The belief of a citizen in any faith or creed shall not be pleaded as an excuse for him to commit

eral Consulate in New York. All quotations used in this study are from that translation.

[24] "33 str. Bažnyčių bei kitų tolygių tikybinių organizacijų padėtis Valstybėje nustatoma susitarimu arba įstatymu."—*VŽ,* No. 608 (1938), 238.

[25] "Valstybė saugo piliečio sąžinės laisvę. . . . Tikintiesiems, kurie yra kieno nors valdžioje, duodama laiko savo tikybos pareigoms atlikti."—*VŽ,* No. 608 (1938), 238.

an offense against, or evade the performance of a duty imposed by the State.[26]

3. Freedom of Communication

As a sequence to the liberty of the Church, acknowledged in Lithuania by the first article of the Concordat, there is the approval for freedom of communication, expressed in the second article as follows:

> The Bishops, the clergy, and the faithful shall have free and direct communication with the Holy See. In the exercise of their functions, Bishops shall communicate freely and directly with their clergy and faithful, and shall likewise be able to publish their instructions, orders and pastoral letters.[27]

The Concordat uses the term "Bishop," but from the text of this article as well as from the manner in which this term is used

[26] "32 str. Valstybės pripažintų bažnyčių bei kitų tolygių tikybinių organizacijų mokslo skelbimas, tikybinių apeigų bei maldų atlikimas ir kita tikybinė veikla, taip pat maldų namai. negali būti naudojami tam, kas priešinga konstitucijai ir įstatymams.

30 str. . . . Piliečio įsitikinimas negali būti pamatas nusikaltimui patesinti arba valstybės dedamai pareigai nevykdyti."—VŽ, No. 608 (1938), 238. The circulars of the Department of Administration on June 13, 1936 forbade the Baptists and Adventists from founding parishes and houses of prayer and from performing religious services without special permission since these sects were not recognized by the state: "Prašoma Tamstų be Švietimo Ministerijos leidimo neleisti nei evangelikams—baptistams, nei septintos dienos adventistams steigti parapijų ar maldos namų, o jų dvasininkams—atlikinėti tikybinių apeigų. Parapijos ir dvasininkai, kurie jau veikia, bet neturi leidimų, privalo juos tuojau pasirūpinti."—*Vidaus Reikalų Ministerijos Administracijos Departamento Aplinkraščiai* (The Circulars of the Department of Administration; Kaunas: Vidaus Reikalų Ministerija, 1938), p. 110. This work cited hereafter as *Administracijos Departamento Aplinkraščiai.*

[27] "Les Evêques, le Clergé et les fidèles communiqueront librement et directement avec Saint-Siège. Dans l'exercice de leurs fonctions, les Evêques communiqueront librement et directement avec leur Clergé et leur fidèles et pourront publier de même leurs instructions, mandements et lettres pastorales."—*AAS,* XIX (1927), 426; A. Perugini, *Concordata Vigentia,* p. 60.

in other articles, it is clear that the term "Bishop" here means "Ordinary," not in the sense of canon 215 § 2,[28] but rather of canon 198.[29]

Freedom of communication means naturally that the State will not hinder the publication and circulation of the decrees of the Pope and of the Ordinaries.[30] By this article the State renounces all claim to any form of interference known in law as the *regium placitum,* or simply the *placet* or *exequatur.*[31]

The Church has always held out strongly against any interference on the part of the state in the freedom of communication.

[28] "In iure . . . venit . . . nomine Episcopi, Abbas vel Praelatus *nullius,* nisi ex natura rei vel sermone contextu aliud constet."

[29] "In iure nomine *Ordinarii* intelliguntur, nisi quis expresse ercipiatur, praeter Romanum Pontificem, pro suo quisque territorio Episcopus residentialis, Abbas vel Praelatus *nullius* eorumque Vicarius Generalis, Administrator, Vicarius et Praefectus Apostolicus, itemque ii qui predictis deficientibus interim ex iuris praescripto aut ex probatis constitutionibus succedunt in regimine, pro suis vero subditis Superiores maiores in religionibus clericalibus exemptis."

Cf. Ottaviani, "Concordatum Lithuanicum" *Apollinaris,* I (1928), 58.

[30] Applying this guarantee of freedom of communication to can. 9 and can. 218 § 2, which deal with the publishing of the decrees of the Holy See, it follows that complete freedom of circulation must be given to the official organ of the Holy See—*Acta Apostolicae Sedis.*—Cf. A. Blat, *Ius concordatarium postbellicum conlatum cum Codice Iuris Canonici* (Romae: Apud "Angelicum," 1938), p. 91. This work hereafter cited as *Ius Concordatarium.*

[31] The Holy See obtained in Lithuania what she could not obtain in the concordat with Russia on August 3, 1847. In the additional protocol ("Articoli non concordati") is found: "Le Cardinal Plénipotentiaire de Sa Sainteté a insisté de donner aux sujets catholiques de S.M. une véritable liberté de communication avec le Saint Siége pour les affaires de conscience, et pour les autres affaires spirituelles.

Les Plénipotentiares de S.M. Impériale ont répondu que le mode actuellement existant pour ces communications, c'est à dire par l'entremise du Gouvernement et de la légation Impériale, avait toujours été maintenu. Les conjunctures actuelles ne permettraient guères au Governement Impérial de se départir de ces mesures de précaution. . . . "—A. Mercati, *Raccolta di Concordati,* p. 761.

The Council of the Vatican, for example, took strong action against the *placet* of the state in Church affairs.[32] There has not been any breach of this norm of the Concordat either in the laws or in their application in Lithuania.[33]

4. *Brachium Saeculare*

The Lithuanian State, by the Concordat, accepted not only negative obligations—to abstain from any interference in the liberty of the Church—but also, in article IV, the positive obligation of giving help:

> The civil authorities shall give their assistance in the execution of ecclesiastical laws and decrees: in the case of an ecclesiastic's divestiture of office or of his deprivation of an ecclesiastical benefice; in the case of the prohibition to wear

[32] Sess. IV., cap. 3, of the Council: "Damnamus ac reprobamus illorum sententias, qui hanc supremi capitis cum pastoribus et gregibus communicationem licite impediri posse dicunt aut eandem reddunt saeculari potestati obnoxiam, ita ut contendant, quae ab Apostolica Sede vel eius auctoritate ad regimen Ecclesiae constituuntur, vim ac valorem non habere, nisi potestatis saecularis placito confirmentur."—The dogmatic Constitution *Pastor Aeternus,* of April 24, 1870.—*ASS,* VI (1870), 44; H. Denzinger, *Enchiridion Symbolorum,* n. 1829. Cf. also alloc. *Luctuosis exagitati,* 12 mart. 1877.—H. Dencinger, *op. cit.,* n. 1847; *ASS,* XI (1878), 605 sq.; *Fontes,* n. 572, § 5. The Church invokes canonical penalties against her members who co-operate with a government which seeks to impede freedom of communication. Cf. canons 2333; 2334; 2336, § 1.

[33] The officials of the State were even instructed to meet the Internuncio or the Bishop at the border of their district and to give him assistance; police had to keep order if a great multitude of people assembled: "Atvykstančius dvasiškos vyriausybės atstovus: internuncijus, ir vyskupus apskrities viršininkas sutinka apskrities miesto ribose, į kurį jie atsilanko oficialiai—vizituodami viskupijas, ar šiaip kuomet atsilankymas viešo pobūdžio . . . Policija dalyvauja tik kaip viešos tvarkos palaikytoja, jei sutikimas ruošiamas skaitlingai miniai dalyvaujant."—*Piliečių Apsaugos Departamento Aplinkraščių Rinkinys* (The Collection of the Circulars of the Department of the Protection of the Citizen; Kaunas: Piliečių Apsaugos Departamentas, 1931), p. 534. Cited hereafter as *Pil. Aps, Depart. Aplinkraščiai.*

the priestly garb; in the case of the collection of taxes destined for Church purposes and permitted by the laws of the State.[34]

This is at least a partial acceptance of the principle of the *brachium saeculare,* mentioned in can. 2198.[35]

The Penal Code of Lithuania enumerates many cases wherein the State protects religion, cult, the Church.[36] In the Concordat, as is evident, the State accepts the triple obligation of assisting in the execution of the punishments or obligations imposed by the Church:

1. In the case in which the ecclesiastic is deprived of an office or benefice, according to canons 192 and 2298, 6°;

2. In the case of a prohibition regarding the wearing of the ecclesiastical garb permanently, as provided by canons 2304, § 1, and 2305, § 1,[37] or temporarily, as provided by can. 2300;[38]

3. In the case of the levying of taxes, as a power that the Church has according to canon 1496.

The Lithuanian Concordat, taking this article from the Polish Concordat, modified it in favor of the Church: it does not repro-

[34] "Les autorités civiles prêteront leur appui à l'éxecution des décisions et des décrets ecclésiastiques: au cas de destitution d'un ecclésiastique ou de sa privation d'un bénéfice ecclésiastique; au cas de défence du port de l'habit ecclésiastiques; au cas de perception des taxes destinées à des buts ecclésiastiques et permises par les lois de l'Etat."—*AAS,* XIX (1927), 426; A. Perugini, *Concordata vigentia,* p. 60.

[35] "Delictum quod unice laedit Ecclesiae legem, natura sua, sola ecclesiastica auctoritas persequitur, requisito interdum. ubi eadem auctoritas nesessarium vel opportunum iudicaverit, auxilio brachii saecularis. . . . "

[36] On January 16, 1919, Lithuania adopted the Penal Code of Russia (*Уголовное Уложеніе,* Высочайше утвержденное 22 марта 1903 года, С.—Петербургъ: Изданіе Государственной Канцеляріи, 1903; hereafter cited as *Уголовное Уложеніе*), which (sections 73-97) includes punishments for blasphemy against the Trinity, the Blessed Virgin, mysteries of the faith, the saints; for crimes and offences against objects of cult, relics; for disturbances during devotions; for forcing a priest to perform any religious act which is forbidden by the Church; for posing as a priest.

Cf. *Lietuvos Įstatymai* (The Laws of Lithuania; I leidinys, Kaunas; A. Merkys ir V. Petrulis), p. 764.

[37] Cf. can 2298, 11°.

[38] Cf. can. 2298, 9°.

duce the restriction that the taxes should be foreseen or foreordained[39] by the civil law. The Lithuanian state countenances all the ecclesiastical taxes except those which fall expressly under the prohibition of the civil law.[40] The Lithuanian Constitution does not include any norms concerning the *Brachium saeculare,* and thus the obligations undertaken by the Lithuanian Government are concessions of the State to the Church.[41]

5. Friendly Relations between the Vatican and Lithuania.

The norms of the Concordat, treated above, deal with the affairs of the Catholic Church in Lithuania itself. Article III states the decisions concerning international diplomatic relations between the Vatican and Lithuania:

> In order to maintain friendly relations between the Holy See and the Lithuanian Republic, an Apostolic Internuncio will reside in Lithuania and a Minister of the Republic will reside at the Holy See.[42]

[39] *Prévues;* the Lithuanian Concordat has the term *permises.*

[40] Cf. "Les Concordats Lithuanien et Letton"—*L'Europe Nouvelle,* X (1928), 118.

[41] The Catholic Church of Lithuania was supported by free offerings, by government grants and by the income from Church property; in Lithuania the Church imposed no taxes on her members as was done, e. g., in Germany.

The State, however, favored the collecting of offerings made to the Church. According to a regulation of the Department of the Protection of the Citizens no permission was needed from civil authority for these collections: "Nr. 108. 1923. XI. 6. Paaiškinama, kad dvasiškiams daryti rinkliavas bažnytiniams reikalams vietinis administracijos leidimas nereikalingas. Bažnytinėse rinkliavose policijos pareiga prižiūrėti, kad nerinktų aukų asmens, nepriklausą prie dvasiškių."—*Pil. Aps. Depart. Aplinkraščiai,* p. 273.

[42] The writer's translation. The original text reads: "Afin de maintenir les relations amicales entre el Saint-Siège et la République de Lithuanie, un Internonce Apostolique résidera en Lithuanie et un Ministre de la République résidera auprès du Saint-Siège."—*AAS,* XIX (1927), 426; A. Perugini, *Concordata vigentia,* p. 60.

The stability of the diplomatic relations was confirmed by the treaty. These relations were and are very desirable, for in the observance of the rules of the Concordat there could arise new questions requiring mutual consultations. Some norms of the Concordat even indicate the requirement of a previous contact on the part of the Vatican with Lithuania, e.g., article XI regarding the consultation with the President before the appointment of the Archbishop or Diocesan Bishops. This serves the purpose to ascertain that the Government has no political objections to the nominee.

Article III of the Concordat agrees with canons 265 and 267, which treat about the Apostolic Delegates, Internuncios, Nuncios. This article likewise corresponds to section 61 of the Lithuanian Constitution, which gave the President power to receive representatives of foreign countries, and to appoint ministers to other sovereigns.[43] The continued practice confirmed the stability of the diplomatic relations foreseen by the Concordat.[44]

[43] "Respublikos Prezidentas reprezentuoja Lietuvos Valstybę. priima svetimųjų valstybių atstovus, skiria Lietuvos atstovus." — *VŽ*, No. 608 (1938), 240.

[44] On May 27, 1928, Msgr. R. Bartoloni was appointed as the Internuncio to Lithuania exclusively.—*AAS*, XX (1928), 209. In 1929 a nunciature was established in Kaunas.

The Lithuanian Telegraph Agency *Elta* in its *Economic and General Bulletin*, No. 7 (1940), 11, giving the latest news before the occupation by the Bolsheviks, issued the following message: "New Papal Nuncio to Lithuania, Monseigneur Luigi Centoza, in April 30 remitted his letters of credence to the President of the Republic, M. Smetona. Having emphasized the great factor of the Catholic religion, with its assurance of happiness to individuals and society, as constituting the most solid foundation for the brotherhood of peoples and a sure guarantee of justice and peace among nations, the Nuncio declared *inter alia:* 'I am animated by the most sincere and ardent desire to co-operate in every way with the true forces for the welfare of your country, to work in order to render always closer and more cordial the good relations which happily exist between Lithuania and the Holy See. From today I shall consider your country as a new Fatherland to me and I ask God ever to preserve for your noble Lithuanian nation the inestimable blessing of peace.'

"In his response President Smetona declared *inter alia:* 'The representative of the Pope in Lithuania is in the midst of a people who, through all the adversities endured during the centuries, have succeeded in preserving the most precious Christian faith in which they have found their power of spiritual and national resistance. The Lithuanian people have equally drawn from the living source of the Catholic religion their faith and their devotion to the ideals of justice, fraternity and peace among nations.' "

The nuncio by the unjust order of the Bolsheviks was forced to leave Lithuania. The Lithuanian Minister St. Girdvainis resides even now at the Vatican.—*Annuario Pontificio per l'Anno 1944* (Città del Vaticano: Tipographia Poliglota Vaticana. 1944), p. 712.

Chapter VIII

THE PRIVILEGES OF THE CLERGY

1. Privilegium Canonis.

The Lithuanian Concordat not only implicitly admits the privileges of the clergy by accepting the right of the Church to follow the norms of the Code, but also explicitly accepts this, as can be gathered from article V of the Concordat.

The first provision of this article states:

> Ecclesiastics shall enjoy special juridical protection in the exercise of their ministry.[1]

By this norm the Concordat, in admitting the proper reverence due to the clergy, provides special protection for them in the exercise of their ministry. It also includes protection against real injury. This stipulation is, at least in part, an acceptance of the Church's law regarding the *privilegium canonis,* as it is expressed in canon 119.[2]

The Concordat here does not mention explicitly the members of the religious communities, as it does in some of the following provisions, but they are included implicitly. *Les ecclésiastiques* is the French term for "clergy." The term *ecclésiastiques* in its meaning of "clergy" is taken from Canon Law, and therein is to be found its explanation. According to canon 614 the religious, even lay brothers and novices, enjoy the privileges of clerics, and even the members of societies of men and women who lead a community life without vows enjoy the privileges of clerics, as follows from canon 680.[3] The State promises a special juridical

[1] "Les ecclésiastique jouiront dans l'exercise de leur ministère d'une protection juridique spéciale."—*AAS,* XIX (1927), 426; A. Perugini, *Concordata vigentia,* p. 60.

[2] Cf. can. 2343.

[3] Cf. interpretation of the similar article of the Polish Concordat by P. Schweiger, "Jus Religiosorum Concordatum pro Polonia"—*CpR,* IX (1928), 122.

protection when clerics exercise their ministry, that is, when they are conducting services, officiating at funerals, leading processions, administering the sacraments, preaching and performing other duties as representatives of the Church. This norm coincides with the provisions of the Penal Code adopted by Lithuania.[4]

The Lithuanian Constitution, by protecting labor, favors protection to persons who perform their duties.[5] Section 18 of the Lithuanian Constitution, however, declares that all citizens of the State shall be equal under the law.[6] The special protection of the clergy, as mentioned above, is to be regarded then as an exception to the general constitutional law. This protection is granted specifically in favor of the Church.[7]

2. Privilegium Competentiae.

The union between Church and State, and the special duties performed by the clergy,[8] made clerics equal to the officials of the State and brought them similar privileges. In article V of the Concordat it is stated:

Like the functionaries of the State, they shall benefit by

[4] *Уголовное Уложеніе,* sections 75-80.

[5] "47 str. Rūpindamasi tikslingu ir taisyklingu piliečių darbo galios sunaudojimu, Valstybė globoja ir rikiuoja darbą."—*VŽ,* No. 608 (1938). 239.

[6] "Prieš įstatymus piliečiai lygūs."—*VŽ,* No. 608 (1938), 238.

[7] Sections 99 and 952 of the Lithuanian law in regard to penal procedure release priests and religious from taking the oath in court. In the case of the condemnation of a clergyman, according to sections 952 and 1028 of the law in regard to penal procedure, the ecclesiastical superiors have to be notified, and before punishment can be inflicted these ecclesiastical superiors must be asked to degrade or depose the delinquent cleric.—G. Gronau, *Das litauische Straf-Prozesz-Gesetz* (German translation by G. Gronau of the law in regard to penal procedure; Memel: G. Gronau, 1934),p p. 35, 231, 248-250.

[8] As, for example, the keeping and issuing of the records of birth, marriage, death.

the right of exemption from judicial seizure for a part of their salaries.[9]

The remuneration of the Lithuanian clergy consisted of the income derived from benefices, from *iura stolae* and from sums paid by the Government.[10] The Concordat allowed that from these revenues a certain percentage could be taken for the payment of debts and similar obligations. But this percentage could not be larger than was allowed by the law in the case of functionaries of the State.[11]

This norm of the Concordat guarantees to the clergy an honest sustenance, which is demanded by canon 122 of the Code of Canon Law. This provision in the Concordat is a concession of the Lithuanian State to the Church.

3. Privilegium Immunitatis.

St. Thomas Aquinas, treating the question of the participation of the clergy in war, affirms that it is unseemly for them to shed blood or to kill. Rather, it is fitting to see them ready to shed

[9] "A l'égal des fonctionnaires de l'Etat, ils bénéficieront du droit d'exemption de la saisie judiciaire pour une partie de leurs traitements."—*AAS*, XIX (1927), 426; A. Perugini, *Concordata vigentia,* pp. 60-61.

[10] The Government paid approximately 25 dollars (150 litas) to deans, 17 dollars (100 litas) to pastors and about 16 dollars (93 litas 33 centas) to assistant pastors every month.—*Švietimo Ministerijos Žinios,* No. 6 (1933), 295. This magazine will be cited hereafter as *ŠMŽ.*

These payments were sent through the Chancery Office, but they were for the most part used by the ecclesiastical superiors for the building and maintenance of seminaries, for the development of the Catholic Action movement, etc.

[11] According to the Russian law (Czarist Russia), accepted by Lithuania, from one-fourth to two-fifths of the income of the functionaries was subject to seizure, depending upon the amount of their monthly revenues.—*Сводъ Законовъ,* vol. XV. sections 1085, 1086.

Ottaviani was not familiar with that legislation when he stated that one-fifth was subject to seizure.—Cf. "Concordatum Lithuanicum,"—*Apollinaris,* I (1928), 59.

their own blood for Christ, and so to imitate in deed what they portray in their ministry.[12]

Many nations accept that principle. It finds approval in the Lithuanian Concordat in article V:

> Ecclesiastics after the reception of orders, religious after pronouncing their vows, seminarians and novices in the novitiates, if they persevere in their ecclesiastical or religious state, shall be exempt from military services, even in the case of war and universal conscription.[13]

The exemption of ecclesiastics from military service by the Concordat is even broader than that granted by the Code of Canon Law. According to canon 121 immunity from military service is granted to clerics,[14] which also includes religious, lay brothers and novices,[15] and the members of societies leading a community life without vows.[16] The Concordat extends immunity also to seminarians, and by analogy, this includes also the postulants of religious communities.[17]

The Lithuanian civil law perfectly coincides with that interpretation. Section 31 of the Constitution declares:

> The clergy of churches recognized by the State shall by law be exempted from military service.[18] The Lithuanian Govern-

[12] "Et ideo non competit eis occidere vel effundere sanguinem, sed magis esse paratos ad propriam sanguinis effusionem pro Christo, ut imitentur opere quod gerunt ministerio."—*Sum. Theol.*, IIa-IIae, q. XL, a. 2.

[13] "Les ecclésiastiques ayant reçu les Ordres, les religieux ayant prononcé leurs voeux, les élèves aux Séminaires et les novices dans les Noviciats, s'ils persévèrent dans leur état ecclésiastique ou religieux, seront exempts du service militaire, même dans le cas de guerre ou de levée en masse."—*AAS*, XIX (1927), 426-427; A. Perugini, *Concordata vigentia*, p. 61.

[14] "Clerici omnes a servitio militari . . . immunes sunt."

[15] Can. 614.

[16] Can. 680. Cf. Cappello, "De Natura Concordatorum"—*JP*, VIII (1928), 16.

[17] Cf. P. Schweiger, "Jus Religiosorum Concordatum pro Polonia"—*CpR*, IX (1928), 124.

[18] "Valstybės pripažintų tikybų dvasininkai įstatymu gali būti atleidžiami nuo tarnavimo kariuomenėje."*VŽ*, No. 608 (1938), 238.

ment on August 25, 1936, promulgated a law in which were enumerated the ecclesiastics of the Catholic Church who are free from military service: 1) Seminarians and candidates of the religious novitiates (postulants); 2) persons who have received tonsure and the four minor Orders, as long as they are preparing to receive Major Orders, and 3) Subdeacons and the clerics in Major Orders.[19] Ecclesiastics, according to the Concordat, are exempt from military service even during war time and in case of universal mobilization. They are not to be called into the military reserves.[20]

The privilege of personal immunity includes also the exemption of ecclesiastics from civil offices and duties which are incompatible with their vocation. Article V of the Concordat has the following provision:

> Ecclesiastics shall be exempt from civil obligations which are incompatible, according to Canon Law, with their sacerdotal office.[21]

The Concordat here fully accepts the norms of Canon Law.[22] The Lithuanian Constitution contains provisions which declare the equality of all citizens[23] and oblige all citizens to participate

[19] "Atleidžiamų nuo karinės prievolės dvasininkų ir dvasinių mokyklų auklėtinių sąrašas:

§ 1. Nuo karinės prievolės atleidžiami:

1. Romos Katalikai: 1) Kunigų seminarijų auklėtiniai ir vienuolijų noviciatų kandidatai—kol yra seminarijoje ar vienuolyne.

2) Asmens, gavę tonsūrą ir keturis mažesniuosius pašventinimus—kol ruošiasi aukštesniems pašventinimams.

3) Subdiakonai ir aukštesnių laipsnių dvasininkai — kol yra dvasininkų luome."—*VŽ*, No. 547 (1936), 2-3.

[20] The interpretation of the Highest Commission of Military Conscription in Lithuania on April 3. 1930, No. 4440.—J. Pukelevičius, *Karinės Prievolės Įstatymas* (The Law of Military Conscription; Kaunas: Neoficialus Piliečių Apsaugos Departamento leidnys, 1931), p. 28.

[21] "Les ecclésiastique seront aussi libérés des fonctions civiques, incompatibles avec la vocation sacerdatale selon le Droit Canon."—*AAS*, XIX (1927), 427; A. Perugini, *Concordata vigentia*, p. 61.

[22] Can. 121. Cf. also canons 138-143.

[23] "18 str.: Prieš įstatymus piliečiai lygūs."—*VŽ*, No. 608 (1938), 238.

in the defense of the country.[24] In view of these provisions the exemption of the clergy in regard to duties which are incompatible with their status, and their exemption from the military service, remain as concessions made by the Lithuanian State to the Church.[25]

4. Privilegium Fori

The Concordat does not as fully acknowledge the *privilegium fori* as it acknowledges the *privilegium immunitatis*. Article XX provides:

> If any ecclesiastics or religious are accused, before lay Tribunals, of crimes provided for by the penal laws of the Republic, said Tribunals shall immediately inform the competent Ordinary of every affair of this kind, and shall transmit to him, if the case warrants it, the formal charge and the judicial decree with the reasons thereof. The Ordinary, or his delegate, shall have the right, after the conclusion of the judicial procedure to take cognizance of the related records. In case of the arrest or imprisonment of the above mentioned persons, the civil authorities shall proceed with due regard for their state and ecclesiastical rank.[26]

Canon 120, in which mention is made of the *privilegium fori*, requires that all cases against clerics, both civil and criminal, be

[24] "133 str.: Valstybę gina visi piliečiai."—*VŽ*, No. 608 (1938), 244.

[25] Ottaviani, mostly having in mind the Constitution of 1922 admits: " . . . vix invenire est aliam Rempublicam in qua et Constitutio et pactum concordatarium tam ampla vestigia immunitatum ecclesiasticarum adhuc servent."—"Concordatum Lithuanicum"—*Apollinaris*, I (1928), 59.

[26] "Si des ecclésiastiques ou religieux sont accusés près des Tribunaux laïque de crimes prévus par les lois penales de la République, ces Tribunaux informeront immédiatement l'Ordinaire compétent de chaque affaire de ce genre et lui transmettront, le cas échéant, l'acte d'accusation et l'arrêt judiciaire avec ses considérants. L'Ordinaire, ou son délégué, auront le droit, après conclusion de la precédure judiciaire, de prendre connaissance des dossiers relatifs. Dans le cas d'arrestation ou d'emprisonement des personnes susmentionnées, les autorités civiles procéderont avec les égards dus à leur état et à leur rang hiérarchique."—*AAS*, XIX (1927), 431; A. Perugini, *Concordata vigentia*, p. 67.

brought into the ecclesiastical court.[27] The Code, however, makes provision for exceptions for particular laws in particular places.[28] An exception has been made in Lithuania by art. XX of the Concordat: ecclesiastics may be brought before lay tribunals in criminal cases, on condition, however, 1) that there be committed an act which has a sanction mentioned in the Criminal Code of Lithuania,[29] and that it be qualified as a crime (felony) by the Penal Code, and not as a simple transgression of law (misdemeanor),[30] and 2) that the ecclesiastics and the religious be ACCUSED before the lay Tribunal.

In all other civil and criminal cases the ecclesiastical tribunal remains exclusively competent to judge ecclesiastical or religious persons, according to can. 1553, § 1.[31] Even in cases of crimes

[27] Can. 120, § 1. "Clerici in omnibus causis sive contentiosis sive criminalibus apud iudicem ecclesiasticum conveniri debent. . . . "

[28] Can. 120, § 1. " . . . nisi aliter pro locis particularibus legitime provisum fuerit."

[29] *Nullum crimen sine lege; nulla poena sine lege.* Cf. The Lithuanian Constitution, section 21; *Уголовное Уложение,* section 1; Law in regard to Penal Process, section 1.

D. (50.16) 131: "Poena non irrogatur nisi quae quaque lege vel alio iure huic delicto imposita est."

See A. Schottlaender, *Die geschichtliche Entwicklung des Satzes: Nulla poena sine lege* (Strafrechtliche Abhandlungen, Heft 132, Breslau: Schletterschc Buchhandlung, 1911) and F. Roberti, *De Delictis et Poenis,* Vol. I, (Romae: Libraria Pontificii Instituti Utriusque Iuris, 1938), p. 69.

[30] According to the Penal Code, article 3, the term "crime," used in the original French text of the Concordat, corresponds to the term *sunkusis nusikaltimas,* and includes those transgressions of laws which have as a punishment condemnation to hard labor.—*Lietuvos Įstatymai,* I leidinys, p. 764, cf. *Уголовное Уложение,* section 3.

[31] Cf. P. Malakauskis, *Viešosios Bažnytinės Teisės,* p. 162; see also the interpretation of the corresponding article of the Polish Concordat by P. Schweiger, "Jus Religiosorum Concordatum pro Polonia"—*CpR,* IX (1928), 126; a similar interpretation is given in a private publication of the Bishops of Poland: *Concordatum cum Republica Polona Initum* (Włocławek: Biuro Episcopatu Polskiego, 1925), p. 102, cited from Wilanowski, "Ustępstwa ze Strony Kosciola na rzecz Panstwa w Konkordacie"—*Rocznik Prawniczy Wilenski,* II (1928), 225-226.

which, according to article XX of the Concordat, will be decided by lay tribunals, the Church does not entirely renounce her right. The State accepts the duty: 1) To inform the proper Ordinary immediately; 2) to transmit to him the formal charge and the juridical decree; and 3) to permit the Ordinary or his delegate to take cognizance of the acts of the case.

The rest of article XX expresses that the State, on account of the *privilegium canonis,*[32] will show respect to the cleric who may have been arrested or even condemned:

> Ecclesiastics and religious will be detained and will serve their punishment in places separated from those of lay men, unless they have been deprived of their ecclesiastical rights by their Ordinary. In case they be condemned to prison by the court, they will serve the punishment in a monastery or other religious house, in the places designated for that purpose.[33]

The Church makes a concession by agreeing that clerics accused of crimes and condemned by lay tribunals may be arrested by the officials of the state and may be detained in places of punishment, separate, however, from those of the lay people.

Article XX of the Concordat was included in the Lithuanian Law of Criminal Procedure as a special norm with reference to the Catholic clergy.[34] The rules given to the police power for the arrest and detention of guilty clerics were in accord with the norms of the Concordat.[35] The Lithuanian civil law countenances

[32] Can. 119.

[33] The writer's translation. Original text: "Les ecclésiastiques et religieux seront détenus et subiront les peines de réclusion dans des locaux séparés des locaux destinés aux laïques, à moins d'avoir été privés par l'Ordinaire compétent de leur dignité d'ecclésiastiques. Au cas où ils seraient condamnés par jugement à la détention, ils subiront cette peine dans un couvent ou autre maison religieuse, en des locaux destinés á cet effet."—*AAS,* XIX (1927), 431; A. Perugini, *Concordata vigentia,* p. 67.

[34] G. Gronau, *Das litauische Straf-Prozesz-Gesetz,* p. 248.

[35] *Nusikaltimams Kelti ir Tirti Vadovėlis* (The Manual for the Investigation and the Prosecution of Crimes, Kaunas: Piliečių Apsaugos Departamentas, 1925), p. 40.

the functioning of the ecclesiastical tribunals, and Lithuanian officials were instructed to co-operate by delivering and executing the decisions of the ecclesiastical judges.[36]

[36] The Precept of the Department of the Protection of Citizens, September 22, 1925: "Įst. rinkinio XI tomo I dal. (kitų tikybų stat.) str. 592, pasakyta, kad asmenims bei jų įgaliotiems, kurie bylai einant turi atvykti konsistorijon, šaukimai tuo reikalu įteikiami konsistorijos nuožiūra ar per jos tarnautojus, arba per atitinkamą vietos administraciją. Ta pačia tvarka persiunčiami kam reikia ir kiti konsistorijos teismo bylose paliepimai.

Tokiu būdu tikybų įstaigų visi teismo raštai gali būti adresatams įteikiami per policiją.

Todėl įsakau policijai pildyti visų tikybų konsistorijų bei kolegijų raštus, liečiančius teismo reikalus."—*Pil. Aps. Depart. Aplinkraščiai*, p. 511.

Chapter IX

THE RIGHT OF APPOINTMENT TO OFFICE

1. The Appointment of the Bishops

A. *Ius Praenotificationis.*

Conditions after World War I were more favorable to the adjustment of the privileges regarding the appointments of Bishops with a view to bringing this into closer conformity with the prescriptions of Canon Law. A comparison of earlier concordats with those of the post-war era makes this evident.[1]

In the Lithuanian Concordat, the provisions concerning the appointment of Bishops are in article XI:

> The choice of Bishops pertains to the Holy See. His Holiness consents to approach the President of the Republic before naming the Archbishop and Diocesan Bishops and Coadjutors *with the right of succession,* so as to make sure that the President has no political objections to a nominee.[2]

The Holy See retains the right to appoint Bishops, as it is expressed in canons 329, § 2, and 350, § 1. An exception is made, however, in regard to the procedure for the appointment of the Archbishop, Diocesan Bishops, and Coadjutors with the right of succession: a concession was granted by the Concordat to the Lithuanian government whereby the State was to be consulted regarding the loyalty of the nominees.

[1] Cf., for example, article XIX of the Concordat with Austria in 1855 (—A. Mercati, *Roccolta di Concordati,* p. 825) and article IV of the concordat with Austria in 1933 (—A. Perugini, *Concordat vigentia,* p. 268; *AAS,* XXVI (1934), 252-253).

[2] "Le choix des Evêques appartient au Saint-Siège. Sa Sainteté consent à s'adresser au Président de la République, avant de nommer L'Archevêque et les Evêques diocésains, les coadjuteurs *cum iure successionis,* pour s'assurer que le Président n'a pas de raisons de caractère politique à soulever contre ce choix."—*AAS,* XIX (1927), 428; A. Perugini, *Concordata vigentia,* p. 63.

The Lithuanian Concordat does not define the meaning of the phrase "political objections," but from the *modus vivendi* with Czechoslovakia it can be deduced that the phrase implies a founded accusation against a candidate on the grounds of his irredentist or separatist political activity directed against the Constitution, against the public order of the country, or against the security of the State.[3] The *ius praenotificationis* as granted to the Lithuanian government does not preclude the right of the Holy See to appoint validly any candidates to the offices mentioned above, as stated in canons 329 and 350.[4]

Article XI of the Concordat abolished the provision of the Russian law inherited by Lithuania, according to which the head of the State claimed the power to appoint the Bishops after consultation with, and approval by the Holy See.[5]

[3] Modus Vivendi inter Sanctam Sedem et Rempublicam Cecosclovachiam, art. IV: "On entend par objections de caractère politique toutes les objections que le Gouvernement serait à même de motiver par des raisons qui ont trait à la sécurité de l'Etat, par example que le candidat choisi se soit rendu coupable d'une activité politique irredentiste, séparatiste ou bien dirigée contre la Constitution ou contre l'ordre publique du pays."—*AAS*, XX (1928), 66; A. Perugini, *Concordata vigentia*, pp. 74-75.

[4] "Mais si une objection politique est produite par l'autorité séculière, le pouvoir religieux remettra l'affaire en considération et devra étudier la valeur des témoignages allégués par le gouvernement civil. Après quoi, gardant toujours le dernier mot en ce domaine des promotions ecclésiastiques, l'autorité religieuse modifiera ou maintiendra son choix final pour la désignation du nouvel évêque."—Yves de la Briére, "La Renaissance Contemporaine du Droit Canonique"—*Revue de Droit International et Legislation Comparée*, XVI (1935), 222-223.

Cf. F. Cappello, "De Natura Concordatorum"—*JP*, VIII (1928), 17: "Episcopi eliguntur a R. Pontifice ad normam can 329, § 2. *Nihil obstat*, de quo in articulo XI, obtinendum a praeside reipublicae nullatenus confundendum est cum *iure* nominandi aut praesentandi ad beneficia consistorialia, vel cum *consensu* praevie exquirendo: utrumque enim excludit praedictus articulus."

[5] *Сводъ Законовъ*, Vol. XI, part I. section 30.

Cf. article XII of the concordat with Russia in 1847.—A. Mercati, *Raccolta di Concordati*, p. 755.

B. *Oath of the Bishops.*

The newly appointed Archbishop, Diocesan Bishops and Coadjutors *cum iure successionis* have to take an oath of fidelity before the President of the State, as provided in article XII of the Concordat:

> The above mentioned Ordinaries, before assuming office, will make an oath of fidelity before the President of the Republic according to the following formula:
>
> "Before God, and upon the Holy Gospels, I swear and promise, as befits a Bishop, fidelity to the Republic of Lithuania. I swear and I promise to respect with the utmost loyalty, and to have my clergy respect the government established by the Constitution. I swear and I promise, further, that I will not take part in any agreement or participate in any counsel capable of bringing harm to the Lithuanian State or to the public order. I will not permit my clergy to participate in such activities. In solicitude for the common good and the interests of the State I shall try to set aside every danger by which I would know the State to be threatened.[6]

The oath of fidelity of the Bishops is a concession of the Church to the State, not treated in the Code, but agreeing with the Church's policy of co-operating with the State,[7] of showing respect

[6] The writer's translation. The original text: "Les Ordinaires ci-dessus, avant d'assumer leurs fonctions, prêteront, entre les mains du Président de la République. un serment de fidélité d'après la formule suivante:

'Devant Dieu et sur les Saints Evangiles, je jure et je promets, comme il convient à un Evêque, fidélite à la République de Lithuanie. Je jure et je promets de respecter en toute loyauté et de faire respecter par mon Clergé le Governement établi par la Constitution. Je jure et je promets en outre que je ne participerai à aucun conseil pouvant porter atteinte à l'Etat lithuanien ou à l'ordre public. Je ne permettrai pas à mon Clergé de participer à de telles actions. Soucieux du bien et de l'intérêt de l'Etat je tâcherai d'en écarter tout danger dont je le saurais menacé."—*AAS*, XIX (1927), 428; A. Perugini, *Concordata vigentia*, p. 63.

[7] Leo XIII in his Encyclical *Cum multa*, December 8, 1882: "Concordiae vero . . . idem est in re Christiana, atque in omni bene constituta

to the constitutional Government,[8] and of avoiding internal discord and disturbances of the public order.[9]

The oath was of rather frequent occurrence in Lithuanian public life: the newly elected President of the State assumed the direction of the government by taking an oath;[10] the Ministers, too, before assuming their duties, had to take an oath.[11] The highest officials of the Church in Lithuania, the Bishops, also had to take the oath according to the laws inherited from Russia.[12] The oath of the Bishops and the conditions for the appointment

reipublica fundamentum; nimirum obtemperatio legitimae potestati, quae iubendo, vetando, regendo, varios hominum animos concordes et congruentes efficit."—*ASS,* XV (1882), 243; *Fontes,* n. 587, §4.

[8] Leo XIII in his Encyclical *Caritatis providentiaeque,* March 19, 1894: "Nihil enim omnino ea [Ecclesia] docet aut praecipit quod maiestati principum, quod incolumitati et progredienti populorum vitae, ullo modo officiat vel adversetur; multa immo ex christiana sapientia assidue profert ad communem eorum utilitatem sane quam conducibilia. In quibus haec memoratu digna: principatum qui teneant, eos imaginem divinae in homines potestatis providentiaeque referre; eorum imperium debere iustum esse et imitari divinum. . . . Qui vero sint sub potestate, debere constanter reverentiam et fidem servare principibus, tamquam Deo regnum per homines exercenti, eisdem obtemperare, *non solum propter iram, sed etiam propter conscientiam* (Rom. XIII, 5), pro ipsis adhibere *obsecrationes, orationes, postulationes, gratiarum actiones* (Tim. III, 1-2); debere sanctam custodire disciplinam civitatis; ab improborum machinationibus sectisque abstinere, nec quidquam facere seditiose; omnia conferre ad tranquillam in iustitia pacem tenendam."—*ASS,* XXVI (1893-1894), 525; *Fontes,* n. 623, §2.

[9] Can. 141, §1. Clerici " . . . neve intestinis bellis et ordinis publici perturbationibus opem quoquo modo ferrant."

Cf. P. Kuraitis, "Konkordatas Šv. Sosto ir Lietuvos Respublikos"—*TK,* IV (1928), 35-56.

[10] The Lithuanian Constitution, Section 65: "Išrinktas Respublikos Prezidentas perima Valstybės vadovavimą, prisiekdamas Tautos atstovų akyvaizdoje."—*VŽ,* No. 608 (1938), 240.

[11] If they were not members of the Church, the oath was replaced by a solemn promise.—Lithuanian Constitution, section 97.—*VŽ,* No. 608 (1938), 242.

[12] *Сводъ Законовъ,* vol. XI, part I, section 31.

of pastors [13] assured the loyalty of the Lithuanian Clergy to the Country and to the Constitutional Government.

2. The Appointments to Benefices, Offices and Institutions

The Concordat, article XVIII, in general accepts the Church's legislation regarding appointments:

> The Republic guarantees the right of competent authorities to assign functions, offices, and ecclesiastical benefices in accordance with the prescriptions of Canon Law.[14]

The terms "ecclesiastical offices" (les charges) and "benefices" (bénéfices) are the classifications of Canon Law, as expressed in canons 145 and 1409. The "functions" (fonctions) denote other ecclesiastical duties not included in the strict definition of offices or benefices. The provision of the Concordat, as stated in the beginning of article XVIII, agrees with the norms of canons 147, 148 and 1431.

The Concordat, however, has an exception in regard to the conferring of benefices:

> In the assignment of the parochial benefices the following rules shall be applied:
>
> In the territory of the Republic of Lithuania the following cannot obtain parochial benefices, unless they have received the consent of the Government: 1° foreigners not naturalized; 2° persons whose activity has been contrary to the security of the State.[15]

[13] ArticleXVIII of the Concordat; treated in the next paragraph of this chapter.

[14] The writer's translation. Original text: "La République guarantit le droit des autorités compétentes d'attribuer les fonctions, les charges et les bénéfices ecclésiastiques d'après les prescriptions du Droit Canon."—*AAS*, XIX (1927), 430; A. Perugini, *Concordata vigentia*, p. 66.

[15] The writer's translation. The original text:

"A l'attribution des bénéfices paroissiaux seront appliquées les règles suivantes:

Dans le territoire de la République de Lithuanie ne peuvent pas obtenir des bénéfices paroissiaux, à moins d'avoir reçu le consentement du Gou-

It is evident from the text of this article that the restrictions apply only in the case of a parochial benefice to be given a priest *in titulum,* that is, as a pastor, according to canon 451. They do not apply in the case of a priest sent to assist or in the case of a substitute to the person appointed as pastor of the benefice;[16] again, they do not affect an ecclesiastic sent temporarily to administer a vacant parish. Even in this case the appointee does not obtain the benefice in the canonical sense; he is only temporarily administering it and taking care of souls. Applying the terminology of the Code, it can be concluded that the Ordinary is entirely free to appoint the administrator of a vacant parish—*vicarium oeconomum* (can. 472, § 1-2) and assistant priests: *vicarium cooperatorem* (can. 476), *vicarium adiutorem* (can. 475) and *vicarium substitutum* (can. 464, § 4).[17]

The Ordinary, before appointing a pastor to a parochial benefice, has to obtain the consent of the Government if the candidate is not a citizen of Lithuania, or if his activity has been contrary to the security of the State. These restrictions, however, cannot be applied to moral persons; therefore, the competent authority is free to unite a parochial benefice to a monastery, to the capitular church or to another moral person, according to the norms of canons 452 and 1423. In that case, according to the requirements of can. 471, § 1, a *vicarius actualis* is to be appointed to the parish. He has all the rights and obligations of the pastor,[18] and, consequently, his appointment is subject to the norms as expressed in article XVIII of the Concordat.[19]

vernement: 1° les étrangers non-naturalisés; 2° les personnes dont l'activité a été contraire à la sécurité de l'Etat."—*AAS,* XIX (1927), 430; A. Perugini, *Concordata vigentia,* p. 66.

[16] Canon Law permits only one pastor in a parish and does not provide for any exceptions. Cf. can. 460, §2.

[17] Cf. P. Malakauskis, *Viešosios Bažnytinės Teisės,* p. 161; J. Labanauskas, "Bažnytinės Pareigavietės" (The Ecclesiastical Offices)—*Draugija,* No. 3 (1939), 218.

[18] Can. 471, § 4. Cf. also can. 451, § 2, n. 2.

[19] Cf. P. Malakauskis. *Viešosios Bažnytinės Teisės,* p. 161.

As is evident from the text, the provisions of this article concern only the appointment of pastors; the loss (*amissio*) of ecclesiastical benefices is not subject to any restrictions and hence will take place according to the norms of canons 183-195 and 1484-1488.

The Ordinary enjoys the freedom to transfer pastors, because 1) there is only a changing of the places of persons whose rights to be pastors are not diminished, and 2) the restrictions of article XVIII speak only of appointments to a benefice, and not of transfers. Moreover, the restrictions are simply exceptions to the general principle of the freedom of the Church in administering ecclesiastical offices or benefices, as stated in the first clause of article XVIII of the Concordat.[20]

The same article likewise provides for the procedure of obtaining the opinion of the Government:

> Before proceeding to nominations to these benefices, the ecclesiastical authority shall make inquiries from the competent Minister of the Republic, to assure itself that none of the reasons foreseen in points one and two stand in the way of the nomination.
>
> In the case wherein the Minister mentioned above will not, during the period of 30 days, have presented such objections against the person to be assigned, the ecclesiastical authority will proceed to the appointment.[21]

The time to answer is limited to 30 days; after that period, if the Minister did not forward his answer—*fatalibus elapsis*—the Ordinary is free to proceed to the appointment.

[20] Cf. J. Labanauskas, "Bažnytinės Pareigavietės"—*Draugija,* No. 2 (1939), 144.

[21] The writer's translation. Original text: "Avant de procéder aux nominations à ces bénéfices, l'autorité ecclésiastique s'informera auprès du Ministre compétent de la République pour s'assurer qu'aucune des raisons, prévues ci-dessus aux points 1. et 2., ne s'y opposerait. Au cas où le Ministre susmentionné ne présenterait pas, dans le délai de 30 jours, de telles objections contre la personne dont la nomination est envisagée, l'autorité ecclésiastique procédera à la nomination."—*AAS,* XIX (1927), 430; A. Perugini, *Concordata vigentia,* pp. 66-67.

The consent to approach the Minister of the State before the appointment to the parochial benefice is a concession of the Church to the State. The restrictions in the appointment to parochial benefices were made in conformity with the Lithuanian law, inherited from Czarist Russia, which requires that only citizens be permitted to hold ecclesiastical offices,[22] and that pastors be appointed only with the consent of the representatives of the Government.[23] The Council of the State, which had the power to interpret the laws of Lithuania,[24] on December 15, 1930, in expressing its respect for the norms of the Concordat, decided however that a religious who as a non-citizen of Lithuania desired a position which brought in revenue had, in accordance with the civil law to request and obtain the permission of the civil authorities.[25] This decision was mostly concerned with the religious who applied for positions as teachers. If these norms were applied in the field of ecclesiastical offices, they would run counter to the regulations of the Concordat.[26]

3. The Lithuanian Military Forces.

The Church's liberty of appointment to ecclesiastical offices was extended to the military forces by article VII which states:

> The armies of the Republic of Lithuania will enjoy all the exemptions accorded to armed forces by the Holy See according to the prescriptions of Canon Law. Chaplains will exercise the duties of their ministry under the jurisdiction

[22] *Сводъ Законовъ,* Vol. XI, part. I, section 54.

[23] *Сводъ Законовъ,* Vol. XI, part I, section 16.

[24] Section 104 of the Lithuanian Constitution.—*VŽ,* No. 608 (1938), 242.

[25] *Pil. Aps. Aplinkraščiai,* pp. 490-492.

[26] There are many examples of perfect co-operation between the two powers. The "instructions" concerning the chaplains of the prisons may be cited as an example. Section 1 of these "instructions" provided that the chaplains be appointed or dismissed by the Bishop with the confirmation of the Minister of Justice.—*TK* (official part), II (1926), 30.

of the Archbishop who will have the right of appointing them.[27]

The Concordat accepts the special ecclesiastical legislation concerning military forces and their chaplains, as provided in canon 451, § 3.[28]

Lithuania did not have a special Bishop for the military forces. The military chaplains were subject to the jurisdiction of the Archbishop of Kaunas, who had the right to appoint them. But there was a Superior Chaplain of the Forces [29] who was, according to the Concordat, also under the jurisdiction of the Archbishop of Kaunas.

The laws of Lithuania [30] provided that the head of the army had to appoint all superiors of the Military Forces. However, the norms of the Concordat made an exception for the appointment of chaplains. The same law, section 17, stated that the Superior Chaplain of the Forces is directly subject to the head of the army.[31] This rule seems to disagree with the norms of the Concordat, according to which the chaplains are to be under the jurisdiction of the Archbishop. In practice, however, there were no difficulties. The chaplain's had other duties besides their purely spiritual ones, for example, they took care of the libraries of the army, and

[27] The writer's translation. Original text: "Les armées de la République de Lithuanie jouiront de toutes les exemptions qui sont accordées aux armées par le Saint-Siège selon les prescriptions du Droit Canon. Les aumôniers exerceront les fonctions de leur ministère sous la juridiction del'Archevêque, qui aura le droit de les choisir."—*AAS,* XIX (1927), 427; A. Perugini, *Concordata vigentia,* p. 61.

[28] "Circa militum capellanos sive maiores sive minores, standum peculiaribus Sanctae Sedis praescriptis."

[29] Cf. The Law concerning Superiors of the Military Forces, section 17. —*VŽ,* No. 465 (1934), 2.

[30] The Law concerning Superiors of the Military Forces, section 18. 7°.—*VŽ,* No. 465 (1934), 2.

[31] "§ 17. Kariuomenės Vado betarpiškai priklauso . . . Vyriausis. Kariuomenės Kapelionas.

§ 18. Kariuomenės Vadas . . . 7) parenka vadus ir viršininkus . . . " —*VŽ,* No. 465 (1934), 1-2.

helped with instructions to the soldiers. In these military affairs they were subject to the officials of the army, but in the care of souls, in purely spiritual matters, they were subject to their ecclesiastical superior only.

The rule of the Lithuanian law concerning the subjection of the Superior Chaplain to the head of the army implies his exemption from the jurisdiction of the lower commanders of the various units of the army.

4. The Patronage.

The participation of patrons in the appointments to ecclesiastical offices by presentation of the candidate is regulated by article XIX of the Concordat:

> The right of patronage either by the State or by private individuals remains in force until a new agreement shall be made. The presentation of a worthy ecclesiastic to a vacant office will be made by the patron within the space of thirty days from a list of three names proposed by the Ordinary. If within the space of thirty days the presentation has not been made, the conferral of the benefice will become free. In the case wherein there is question of a parochial benefice, the Ordinary, before proceeding to the nomination, will consult the competent Minister conformably to article XVIII.[32]

Patronage is accepted by Canon Law in canon 1448. Canons 1448-1471 contain norms elaborated in detail. The provision of the Concordat which states that the patron has to select from the

[32] The writer's translation. Original text: "Le droit de patronage, soit de l'Etat soit particuliers, reste en vigueur jusqu'à un nouvel accord. La présentation d'un digne ecclésiastique au poste vacant sera effectuée par le patron dans le délai de 30 jours sur une liste de trois noms proposée par l'Ordinaire. Si dans les 30 jours la présentation n'a pas été faite, la provision du bénéfice deviendra libre. Dans le cas où il s'agirait d'un bénéfice paroissial, l'Ordinaire. avant de procéder à la nomination, consultera le Ministre compétent conformément à l'article XVIII."—*AAS*, XIX (1927), 431; A. Perugini, *Concordata vigentia,* p. 67.

three candidates proposed by the Ordinary corresponds to the enactment of canon 1452.

The Concordat, however, insists on a restriction which is more favorable to the Church than the enactment of the Code. Canon 1457 allows the patron a period of four months for presenting a candidate from those proposed by the Ordinary. The Concordat reduces this period of time to one month.

As a matter of fact, there was actually no right of patronage extant in any place in Lithuania.[33] The provisions concerning patronage were introduced into the Lithuanian Concordat in imitation of the provisions contained in the Polish Concordat,[34] and, probably, because of the influence of the Russian laws, which had provisions concerning patronage.[35]

[33] Cf. P. Malakauskis, *Viešosios Bažnytinės Teisės,* p. 162.

[34] Article XXI.—*AAS,* XVII (1925), 280; A. Perugini, *Concordata vigentia,* p. 43.

[35] *Сводъ Законовъ,* Vol. XI, part I, sections 176-181.

Chapter X

THE JURIDICAL PERSONS OF THE CHURCH

1. Recognition of Rights.

The first article of the Concordat, recognizing the liberty of the Church,[1] admits the right of jurisdiction of the Church, the right to administer property, and the right to conduct her affairs according to Divine and Canon Law. This provision includes recognition of the juridical personality of the Church and her institutions, as stated in Canon Law. In other articles of the Concordat, which will be treated later, there are norms which indicate recognition also for juridical persons in the Church. For example, the State recognizes the right of property as pertaining to juridical ecclesiastical or religious persons,[2] and the Government likewise recognizes the ownership of all goods possessed by the juridical persons of the Church during the signing of the Concordat.[3] These clear expressions show that by the Concordat the juridical personality of the Church and of her institutions is recognized as the principles of Canon Law demand. The Code instead of employing the term "juridical person," uses the term *"persona moralis."* The basic norms governing moral persons are to be found in canons 99-106.

The Lithuanian Republic countenances the recognition of the juridical personality of the Church and her institutions:

Section 30: The Churches and other confessional organizations recognized by the State shall enjoy the rights of juri-

[1] See part II, chapter VII, section 2 of this study.

[2] Article XVII: "Toutes les personnes juridiques ecclésiastiques et religieuse ont . . . le droit d'acquérir . . . leurs biens . . . "—*AAS*, XIX (1927). 430; A. Perugini, *Concordata vigentia*, p. 66.

[3] Articles XXII: "La République de Lithuanie reconnaît les droits de propriété des personnes juridiques ecclésiastiques et religieuses à tous les biens . . . que ces personnes juridiques possèdent actuellement . . . "—*AAS*, XIX (1927), 431; A. Perugini, *Concordata vigentia*, p. 68.

dical persons. The limits of these rights shall be defined by law.[4]

According to section 33 of the Constitution, which admits the principle of agreement in determining the status of the Church,[5] the law which defines the limits of the rights of juridical persons in the Catholic Church is the Concordat, the norms of which accept the regulations of the Canon Law.

2. The Dioceses

The Lithuanian Government, which towards the end of 1926 was Leftist and later became Nationalist, did not want to recognize and acknowledge full rights for the newly formed dioceses of Kaišedorys and Vilkaviškis. The reason adduced was that these dioceses were formed from the territories of Vilnius and Seinai, which at the time were included in the Polish ecclesiastical province.

The problem was solved by article IX of the Concordat:

> No part of the Republic of Lithuania shall be subject to a Bishop whose see is outside the Lithuanian State. The ecclesiastical province, the dioceses and the prelacy of which were fixed by the Bull *Lithuanorum gente,* shall not be modified without previous agreement with the Lithuanian Government, excepting the adjustment of parishes necessary for the good of souls. In any event, the limits of the ecclesiastical province, the dioceses, the prelacy shall conform with the frontiers of the Lithuanian State.[6]

[4] "Valstybės pripažintos bažnyčios bei kitos tolygios tikybinės organizacijos turi teisinio asmens teisių. Šių teisių ribos nustatomos įstatymu." —*VŽ,* No. 608 (1938), 238.

[5] "Bažnyčių bei kitų tolygių tikybinių organizacijų padėtis Valstybėje nustatoma susitarimu arba įstatymu."—*VŽ,* No. 608 (1938), 238.

[6] "Aucune partie de la République de Lithuanie ne dépendra d'un Evêque dont le siège se trouverait en dehors des frontières de l'Etat lithuanien. La Province ecclésiastique, dont les diocèses et la prélature sont fixés par la Bulle Lithuanorum gente, ne sera modifiée san accord préalable

By this article, the Apostolic Constitution *"Lituanorum Gente"*[7] became the *bulla concordata,* and the Lithuanian Ecclesiastical Province was officially recognized by the Government. The Church accepted the obligation not to undertake any additional important modifications of the boundaries of dioceses or of the prelature without previous agreement with the Government. This is one of the concessions made by the Church to the State, for, according to can. 215, § 1, any adjustment in regard to ecclesiastical provinces, dioceses, or prelatures *nullius* is the exclusive right of the supreme power of the Church.

This article of the Concordat brought satisfaction to the Lithuanian Government, for, if the district of Vilnius[8] and Seinai should again be included in the Lithuanian State, they would also be included in the Lithuanian Ecclesiastical Province, since "the limits of the ecclesiastical province . . . shall conform with the frontiers of the Lithuanian State."[9]

3. Parishes, Religious Orders and Congregations

After the decisions concerning the ecclesiastical province and the dioceses, the Concordat provides the norms for smaller territorial and organizational units of the Church. Article X states:

avec le Gouvernement lithuanien, sauf les rectifications paroissiales exigées par le bien des âmes. En tout cas les limites de la Province ecclésiastique, des diocèses et de la prélature seront conformes aux frontières de l'Etat lithuanien."—*AAS,* XIX (1927), 427; A. Perugini, *Concordata vigentia,* p. 62.

[7] See part I, chapter V of this study.

[8] The Lithuanian Constitution, section 6, still has a provision that Vilnius is the capital of Lithuania.—*VŽ,* No. 608 (1938), 237.

[9] The Church is inclined to have the limits of dioceses and of ecclesiastical provinces coincide with the limits of the State.

As A. Maser (*Das Konkordat zwischen dem Apostolischen Stuhle und der Republik Litauen vom 27 September* 1927 *in rechtsvergleichender Betrachtung,* p. 21) states: "Man darf sagen, dasz dem Bestreben von staatlicher Seite, die Diözesangrenzen mit den Staatsgrenzen in Einklang zu bringen, von der Kirche mehr und mehr nachgegeben wird."

> The erection and modification of ecclesiastical benefices, of Congregations and Religious Orders, as well as of their houses and establishments, will pertain to competent ecclesiastical authority which, whenever the above mentioned measures entail expense to the State Treasury, will proceed thereto after an understanding with the Government.[10]

Thus the Church has full freedom for the erection and modification of benefices, as provided in canons 1414-1418 and canons 1419-1430. The Concordat recognizes the freedom of the Church in the erection or modification of religious Orders and Congregations,[11] as well as of their houses, according to the norms of canons 492-498. The same freedom is admitted for the erection and modification of their institutions, such as schools, hospitals and similar institutes, according to canon 497, § 3, which is in agreement with the Lithuanian Constitution, section 60.

There is, however, one exception to the complete freedom of the Church. It concerns the financial side: If the erection or modification should require subsidies from the Treasury of the State, a previous agreement with the Government is necessary. In Lithuania, the State paid the salaries of the priests laboring in the parishes, and granted subsidies for institutions with educational purposes.[12] In these and similar cases the consent of the Government was necessary.

The remaining part of the article contains special provisions concerning Religious Orders and Congregations:

[10] The writer's translation. Original text: "La création et la modification des bénéfices ecclésiastiques, des Congrégations et Ordres religieux, ainsi que de leurs Maisons et établissements, dépendra de l'autorité ecclésiastique compétente, laquelle, toutes les fois que les dites mesures entraineraient des dépenses pour de Trésor de l'Etat, y procédera après entente avec le Gouvernement."—*AAS,* XIX (1927), 427; A. Perugini, *Concordata vigentia,* p. 62.

[11] This includes the freedom to organize a province of the religious community. — Cf. P. Schweiger, "Jus Religiosorum Concordatum pro Polonia"—*CpR* VIII (1927), 463.

[12] Cf. Malakauskis, *Viešosios Bažnytinės Teisės,* p. 156.

Congregations and Religious Orders will have the full right to establish themselves and to exist in Lithuania, if in the Republic they constitute a province according to the norms of Canon Law.

If they do not fulfill this condition but are already existing in the territory of the State, the houses existing at the moment of the ratification of the present Concordat will be recognized by the State; however they shall not be able to open new houses without special authorization of the Holy See.[13]

The Concordat accepts all the rules of Canon Law regarding the establishment and existence of Orders and Congregations except that such Orders and Congregations must constitute a province in Lithuania itself. This exception is a concession on the part of the Church to the State, which does not want its citizens to be subject to the provinces of foreign countries.[14]

Acknowledging those Orders and Congregations which already existed in Lithuania at the moment of the ratification of the Concordat, even though they were not organized into provinces, article X lays down a restriction: they may erect new houses only by special authorization of the Holy See. This means that even religious communities which are subject to the jurisdiction of the

[13] The writer's translation. Original text: "Les Congrégations et Ordres religieux pourront de plein droit s'établir et exister en Lithuanie s'ils constituent dans la République une province selon les règles du Droit Canon.

S'ils ne remplissent pas cette condition et déjà ils existent dans le territoire de l'Etat, les maisons existantes au moment de la ratification du présent Concordat seront reconnus par l'Etat. cependant ils ne pourront pas ouvrir des maisons nouvelles sans une autorisation spéciale du Saint-Siège."—*AAS*, XIX (1927), p. 428; A. Perugini, *Concordata vigentia*, p. 63.

[14] In view of the fact that the territory and the population of Lithuania is not large, there is hope for the establishment and existence of only such Orders and Congregations as will enjoy great popularity with the people and as can be organized into a province.

Cf. B. Wilanowski, "Stosunek Kosciola do Państwa w swietle ostatnich Konkordatów"—*Rocznik Prawniczy Wileński*, IV (1930), 200.

Ordinary, in order to erect a new house, must apply for permission from the Holy See. Since this is an exception to canon 492, § 2, it is a kind of concession made by the Church.

The Lithuanian Constitution countenances the freedom of the activities of the religious Orders, Congregations and even Fraternities:

> Section 29. Religious orders, congregations, and fraternities belonging to the churches or other confessional organizations recognized by the State shall enjoy freedom of action in so far as their activities shall be confined to the teaching of religious beliefs and the performance of ceremonies and acts of worship.[15]

4. The Right to Acquire and to Administer Property.

As a consequence of the recognition of the rights of ecclesiastical juridical persons comes their right to hold property, which right is now confirmed by the treaty, as is expressed in article XVII of the Concordat:

> All juridical ecclesiastical and religious persons have, according to the norms of common law, the right to acquire, dispose of, possess and administer in accordance with Canon Law property both real and personal, as well as the right to appear before every court or authority of the State to defend their civil rights.[16]

This provision of the Concordat, as G. Lampis[17] states, has a

[15] "Valstybės pripažintų bažnyčių bei kitų tolygių tikybinių organizacijų dvasiniai ordinai, kongregacijos ir brolijos, kiek jų veikla pasireiškia tikybos mokslo skelbimu ir tikybinėmis apeigomis bei maldomis, gali veikti laisvai."—*VŽ,* No. 608 (1938), 238.

[16] "Toutes les personnes juridiques ecclésiastiques et religieuses ont, selon les règles du droit commun, le droit d'acquérir, de céder, de posséder et d'administrer, conformément au Droit Canon, leurs biens meubles ou immeubles, de même que le droit d'ester devant toute instance ou autorité de l'Etat pour la défense de leurs droits civils."—*AAS,* XIX (1927), 430; A. Perugini, *Concordata vigentia,* p. 66.

[17] "Il Concordato tra la Santa Sede e lo Stato Lituano"—*Rivista di Diritto Publico,* XXI (1929), p. 232.

great similarity to that of canon 1495, § 2.[18] In regard to property the Concordat accepts the same rights of juridical ecclesiastical and religious persons as are expressed in the Code of Canon Law, that is, the Concordat admits the right to acquire, to dispose of, to possess, and to administer property not only in favor of religious persons (canons 531-532)[19] and associations (canon 691) but also of other ecclesiastical juridical persons,[20] according to the norms contained in canons 1495-1551.

Accepting the legislation of Canon Law regarding the right of property as pertaining to the juridical persons of the Church, the Concordat implicitly accepts also the exceptions which are provided in the Code; for example, regarding the acquisition of ecclesiastical goods by prescription, as stated in canons 1509-1511.[21] Although allowing special provisions and exceptions of Canon Law to be followed, the Concordat requires, however, that in general the norms of the Common Law should be observed, which demand is in conformity with the legislation of canons 1508, 1523, § 2, and 1529. Article XVII of the Concordat recognizes also the right of the juridical persons of the Church "to appear before every court or authority of the State to defend their civil rights." This makes the juridical or administrative procedure available to them, which is in agreement with the law of canons 1646 and 1649.

The civil law of Lithuania approves the right of the juridical persons of the Church in regard to property.[22] The Concordat even abolished the restrictions which were imposed by the Russian legislation upon the ecclesiastical juridical persons in regard to

[18] " . . . personis moralibus quae ab ecclesiastica auctoritate in iuridicam personam erectae sint, ius est. ad normam sacrorum canonum, bona temporalia acquirendi, retinendi et administrandi."

[19] In regard to the rights of religious communities. attention and consideration are to be given to the constitutions which have been approved by the proper ecclesiastical authorities.

Cf. P. Schweiger, "Jus Religiosorum Concordatum pro Polonia,"—*CpR*, IX (1928), 346.

[20] Cf. can. 99; 100.

[21] Cf. P. Malakauskis, *Viešosios Bažnytinės Teisės*, p. 161.

[22] *Сводъ Законовъ*, Vol. X, part I, sections 413, 698, 984, 1067, 1429, 1430.

property.[23] The norm of the Concordat, as expressed in article XIII, was accepted by the judicial and administrative organs of the State. For example, the Highest Tribunal of Lithuania approved it on March 8-22, 1937, by adopting the decision: the right of the religious to inherit goods for the sake of his community must be accepted according to the Code of Canon Law and the Constitution of that religious community.[24] The courts of Lithuania likewise admit the right of the juridical persons of the Church to acquire property by prescription.[25]

[23] *Сводъ Законовъ* Vol. XI, part 1, sections 113, 117.

[24] P. V. Raulinaitis, "Bažnyčia, Kaipo Juridinis Asmuo" (The Church as a Juridical Person)—*Draugija,* No. 12 (1940), 565.

[25] Cf. P. V. Raulinaitis, "Nekilnojamųjų Turtų Nuosavybės Dokumentų Sutvarkymas" (The Obtaining of the Documents regarding Real Estate) —*Draugija,* No. 2 (1940), 110.

Chapter XI

MARRIAGES AND THE PRESERVATION AND ISSUING OF VARIOUS RECORDS

1. Marriages.

Independent Lithuania was one of the few countries in Europe where the Catholic form of marriage enjoyed full recognition by the State. Article XV of the Concordat provides:

> Marriages celebrated in conformity with Canon Law shall *ipso facto* obtain full civil effects.[1]

The Concordat approves for Catholics not only the form of marriage as enacted in canon 1094, but also all the rules promulgated in the Code in canons 1012-1142.[2] If the State admits full civil effects for marriages celebrated in conformity with the Code, it is evident that the State has to accept the competence of the Church to judge concerning contracts of marriage concluded according to her laws; by article XV of the Concordat the State implicitly accepts the exclusive competence of the tribunals of the Church in cases of marriage contracted according to her norms.[3]

The laws of the State approve such an interpretation of article XV. The Lithuanian Constitution protects the stability of the family:

[1] "Les mariages célébrés en conformité des prescriptions du Code Canonique obtiennent par là même les effets civils."—*AAS,* XIX (1927), 429; A. Perugini, *Concordata vigentia,* p. 65.

2 "Itemque optima omnique laude celebranda dispositio art. XV, qui statuit matrimonia inita secundum formam a Codice iuris canonici praefinitam, *eo ipso* valida esse etiam coram Statu omnesque effectus civiles sortiri. Faxit Deus ut etiam in Italia, in Gallia, ubique gentium, hoc praescriptum ipso iure divino exigente. vim obtineat!"—F. Cappello, "De Natura Concordatorum"—*JP,* VIII (1928), 17.

Cf. G. Lampis, "Il Conocrdato tra la S. Sede e lo Stato Lituano"—*Rivista di Diritto Publico,* XXI (1929), 230: "Per ciò che concerne la forma degli atti, si osservano le norme del Rituale Romano e quelle che l'Ordinario stimerà di impartire."

[3] Cf. Ottaviani, "Concordatum Lithuanicum,"—*Apollinaris,* I (1928). 63.

Section 34. The unity of the family shall be recognized as the source of the strength of the State. The State shall respect, protect, and safeguard the family. Large families shall be held in particular honor.[4]

The Lithuanian civil law, inherited from Czarist Russia, qualifies marriage not only as a civil contract, but sees in it an act of religion, recognizes the sacramental character of the contract, and admits the Church's full power to regulate the marriages of her members.[5] Church marriages, according to the civil law inherited from Russia, were obligatory in Independent Lithuania.[6] In practice there were no civil marriages in Lithuania proper.[7]

The civil law admitted the competence of the ecclesiastical tribunals in cases of marriage.[8] If a marriage case was brought before the civil courts, the secular judges had to ask for the decision of the ecclesiastical court concerning the theological and canonical points involved, and only then, in view of that decision, could the mere civil effects of the marriage be settled.[9] A verdict

[4] "Tvirta šeima yra Valstybės stiprumo pamatas. Valstybė gerbia, saugo ir globoja šeimą. Gausios šeimos ypatingai globojamos."—*VŽ,* No. 608 (1938), 238.

[5] Cf. L. Maser, *Das Konkordat zwischen dem Apostolischen Stuhle und der Republik Litauen vom 27 September* 1927 *in rechtsvergleichender Betrachtung,* p. 25.

[6] *Сводъ Законовъ,* Vol. X, part I, section 65: "Браки лицъ всѣхъ вообще Христіанскихъ исповѣданій должны быть совершаемы по ихъ закону духовенствомъ той Церкви, къ которой принадлежатъ вступающіе въ супружество . . ."
Cf. *Сводъ Законовъ,* Vol. X, part I, section 61.

[7] In the district of Klaipėda, where the German Code (*BGB*) was in power civil marriages were obligatory. Cf. M. Kavolis, *Bažnytinės Tikybiniai Mišriosios ir Civilinės Moterystės Juridinė Padėtis Lietuvoje* (The Juridical Situation of Mixed and Civil Marriages in Lithuania; Kaunas: M. Kavolis, 1930), p. 11. This work hereafter cited as *Moterystės Padėtis Lietuvoje.*

[8] *Сводъ Законовъ,* Vol. XI. part I, section 64.

[9] The Law of Penal Procedure, sections 1012-1015; cf. section 1016. —G. Gronau, *Das litauische Straf-Prozesz-Gesetz,* pp. 246-248.

of the Highest Tribunal of Lithuania, on November 1, 1935, recognized the civil effects of a decision of the ecclesiastical court which dissolved a marriage through the application of the Pauline Privilege.[10] The civil law, however, did not agree with the rule of canon 1960 in the Canon Law Code in regard to mixed marriages. For example, in a case where a mixed marriage was celebrated successively before the minister of both contracting parties, the validity and legality of that marriage had to be judged by the tribunal of the Church of the minister before whom it was first contracted.[11] This was the procedure even when the second celebration was a case of convalidation in the Catholic Church.

As has been said above, for marriages in Lithuania the juridical form of the Church is obligatory. But an exception is made for the citizens of Lithuania living abroad. A circular of the Foreign Minister, on June 12, 1924, No. 8775, permitted them under certain conditions to contract marriage, and to register deaths, baptisms, etc., in any Church or civil institution of the country where they reside.[12]

2. Records of Birth, Baptism, Marriage, and Death.

A particular example of the co-operation between Church and State is found in article XIV of the Concordat:

> The clergy in Lithuania shall be entitled to keep registers of birth, baptism, marriage, and death which, conformably

[10] P. Raulinaitis, "Bažnyčia. Raipo Juridinis Asmuo"—*Draugija*, No. 12 (1940), 563.

[11] *Сводъ Законовъ*, Vol. X, part I, section 74.

[12] "Liet. Valstybės Konst. § 3 ir § 13 prasmėje civiliniai aktai, padaryti Lietuvos piliečių užsienyje, einant veikiančiais apsigyvenimo šaly įstatymais gali būti laikomi teisėtais Lietuvoj, nors šie aktai yra atlikti ne pas atatinkamos konfesijos dvasininkus ir be bažnytinių šios konfesijos apeigų, todėl Lietuvos Atstovybės ir Konsulatai gali tokius gimimo, mirimo, jungtuvių etc. metrikus legalizuoti ir taikinti jų savininkams visas iš to legalizavimo paeinančias teises."—M. Kavolis, *Moterystės Padėtis Lietuvoje*, p. 56.

> to the Constitution of the country,[13] shall be accepted as evidence in the civil courts.[14]

This norm agrees with the provisions of the Code regarding the records of baptisms (canons 470 and 777), of marriages (canons 470 and 1103), and of deaths (canons 470 and 1238).

The State recognizes the records issued by the Church as valid documents in public life, and the Church accepts the obligation to provide the State with the records, as expressed in the second part of this article:

> The Church provides the State with copies of the records of the current year, as well as with the records which correspond to the year of levy or conscription. In the case wherein the work entailed with the records is not compensated by the parties concerned, the State will provide remuneration.[15]

The norms of article XIV correspond to the civil law of Lithuania, according to which the Church has to keep records and at certain times has to send a copy of them to the civil institutions.[16]

[13] The Lithaunian Constitution of 1922, which was in force during the time when the Concordat was concluded, stated: "Section 85. Birth, marriage or death certificates, made by the faithful before their spiritual advisers, if they comply with the form determined by law, shall have legal force in Lithuania, and citizens shall not be compelled to repeat such acts in another institution."

[14] "Le Clergé, en Lithuanie, est authorisé à tenir des registres de naissance et de baptême, de mariage et de décès, qui, conformément à la Constitution du pays, font foi même dans le for civil."—*AAS,* XIX (1927), 429; A. Perugini, *Concordata vigentia,* p. 65.

The words " . . . le for civil" are translated in Cicognani's book *Canon Law,* p. 474, as "civil courts." The meaning of "le for civil" is even broader; in this case it means—civil courts and public life, public institutions in general. This is the way it was interpreted in the official translation by the Lithuanian Government. Cf. *VŽ,* No. 264 (1927), 4.

[15] Translated by the writer. Original text: "L'Eglise fournit à l'Etat des copies des registres de l'année en cours, ainsi que les registres de levée de l'année corespondante. Si le travail de la rédaction des actes n'est pas payé par les intéressés eux-mêmes, l'Etat le rétribuera."—*AAS,* XIX (1927), 429; A. Perugini, *Concordata vigentia,* p. 65.

[16] *Сводъ Законовъ,* Vol. XI, sections 883, 884, 888.

The Church records, even according to civil law, serve as a main or primary proof in marriage cases in the civil court.[17]

In the years 1937-1940 the question of introducing into Lithuania a civil system of records was much discussed. The new Constitution (1938) already made the necessary provisions concerning the new legislation:

> Section 125. Records of births, marriages, and deaths shall be prepared by the State authorities in accordance with the procedure and on the conditions determined by law.[18]

Catholics, however, not only by the Concordat, but also by the Constitution, were assured that their rights regarding records would be recognized in this new arrangement, as stated in another part of the same section of the Constitution:

> Persons who are members of a religious denomination shall be free to have such records prepared by their own ministers on the conditions and in accordance with the procedure determined by law, and are not obliged to have them prepared again elsewhere.[19]

[17] *Сводъ Законовъ,* Vol. X, part I, section 34.

[18] "Gimimo, jungtuvių ir mirimo aktai daromi valstybės organų įstatymo numatytomis sąlygomis ir tvarka."—*VŽ,* No. 608 (1938), 243.

[19] "Tikintieji šiuos aktus gali daryti pas savo dvasininkus įstatymo numatytomis sąlygomis ir tvarka ir neverčiami jų kartoti kitur."—*VŽ,* No. 608 (1938), 244.

The translation as given above was made by the officials of the Consulate General of Lithuania in New York. The word "records" in the original text is "aktai"—"acts." It is implied that the Government will recognize not only records of the Church, but also acts, such as the contraction of marriages.

Chapter XII

SACRED PLACES AND TIMES; THE RIGHT TO ONE'S NATIVE LANGUAGE

1. Churches, Chapels and Cemeteries.

Besides the provisions regarding personal immunity,[1] the Concordat contains, in article VI, norms concerning the immunity of sacred places (*immunitas localis*):

> Immunity is granted to Churches, chapels, and cemeteries, so far as is consistent with public safety.[2]

From this it follows that sacred places in Lithuania are under ecclesiastical jurisdiction, which is in conformity with canon 1160.[3] An exception is made in the Concordat in regard to cases wherein danger to public safety impends, for example, if during a time of war the enemy should concentrate its troops in a church or in a cemetery.[4] According to this norm of the Concordat, there is acknowledged the *ius asyli* in regard to sacred places, as far as the public safety permits. But the privilege of the *ius asyli* as expressed in the Concordat is not as extensive as that provided for by canon 1179. Immunity is extended to churches,[5] to cemeteries [6] and to chapels. The Concordat does not specify any type of chapel, and so the right of immunity is conceded to both public and semi-public, and even to private chapels.[7] The acknowledge-

[1] See part II, chapter VIII, of the study.

[2] "L'immunité des églises, des chapelles et des cimetières est assurée, sans que cependant la sécurité publique ait à en souffrir."—*AAS*, XIX (1927), 427; A. Perugini, *Concordata vigentia;* p. 61.

[3] "Loca sacra exempta sunt a iurisdirtione auctoritatis civilis et in eis legitima Ecclesiae auctoritas iurisdictionem suam libere exercet."

[4] Cf. P. Malakauskis, *Viešosios Bažnytinės Teisės,* p. 155.

[5] Cf. can. 1161.

[6] Cf. can. 1206.

[7] Cf. can. 1188.

ment of the immunity of sacred places includes the admission of the right of the ecclesiastical authorities to build churches and chapels, to have their own cemeteries, and to administer these matters according to the rules of Canon Law, and according to the civil norms set up regarding public safety.[8]

The civil law of Lithuania is in agreement with the provisions of the Concordat. The Lithuanian Constitution, section 28, states:

> The Churches . . . shall be allowed freely to . . . maintain their places of worship.[9]

The profanation of a cemetery is punished by the state.[10] The State extends immunity even to monasteries and to the official buildings of the Bishop; in case of search, the officials of the State have to contact the competent ecclesiastical superior in advance.[11]

In practice, immunity is extended to the enclosed property on which the Church is located;[12] but any meeting, if called in these places, has to be held according to the norms of the civil law, as required by the authorities of the State.[13]

2. Holy Days.

The Lithuanian Concordat does not present a list of the holy days of the Church which have been accepted by the State, as does the Italian [14] or the Austrian [15] Concordat.

[8] Cf. P. Schweiger, "Jus Religiosorum Concordatum pro Polonia"—*CpR*, VIII (1927), 463.

[9] "Valstybės pripažintos bažnyčios . . . gali laisvai . . . turėti maldų namus."—*VŽ*, No. 608 (1938). 238.

[10] *Уголовное Уложение*, section 79.

[11] G. Gronau, *Das litauische Straf-Prozess-Gesetz*, p. 111.

[12] Close, curtilage; Lithuanian term—*šventorius.*

[13] The Law for Meetings and Amusements, and The Circular of the Minister of Home Affairs, April 18, 1931, No. 21522.—*Administracijos Departamento Aplinkraščiai*, p. 100.

[14] Article XI.—*AAS*, XXI (1929), 279; A. Perugini, *Concordata vigentia*, pp. 118-119.

[15] Article IX.—*AAS*, XXVI (1934), 260; A. Perugini, *Concordata vigentia*, p. 280.

The Lithuanian Concordat, however, has a provision for special prayers to be said on holidays:

> Article VIII. On Sundays and on the National Fête of Independence, the officiating priest shall recite a liturgical prayer for the prosperity of the Republic of Lithuania and its President.[16]

The prayers for the Country and the President have value not only as an act of cult and as an expression of patriotism, but also as a factor enhancing the authority of the President and of the Government. And this is a concession of the Church to the State. In some way this provision of the Concordat includes recognition of the National Feast of the State[17] by the Church, and also recognition of the Church's holy days[18] by the State.

The Lithuanian Constitution countenances the spiritual character of holidays:

> Section 10. National holidays, Sundays, and other holidays that may be recognized by the State shall be days of rest and spiritual contemplation.
>
> Work on holidays shall be authorized in such cases as are provided for by law.[19]

All Catholic holy days were recognized by law as holidays throughout the country.[20]

The Concordat does not include the text of the liturgical prayer to be said for the Republic and the President, but in a conference

[16] "Les dimanches et le jour de la fête nationale de l'indépendance les prêtres officiants réciteront une prière liturgique pour la prosperité de la République de Lithuanie et de son Président."—*AAS,* XIX (1927), 427; A. Perugini, *Concordata vigentia,* p. 62.

[17] Cf. Constitution of Lithuania, section 9.—*VŽ,* No. 608 (1938), 237.

[18] Can. 1247.

[19] "Valstybės šventės, sekmadieniai ir kitos Valstybės pripažįstamos šventės yra poilsio ir dvasinio pakilimo dienos.

Šventėse gali būti dirbama įstatymu nustatytais atvejais."—*VŽ,* No. 608 (1938), 237.

[20] Law of Holidays and Days of Rest, sections 1-2.—*VŽ,* No. 328 (1930), 2-3.

the Bishops of Lithuania selected it.[21] According to the decision of the Lithuanian Bishops, the prayer has to be said immediately after the main devotions.[22]

[21] The prayer accepted by the Bishops is in the liturgical language of the Church, that is. in Latin:

V. Salvam fac Rempublicam nostram, Domine,
R. Et exaudi nos in die, qua invocaverimus Te,
V. Mitte ei, Domine, auxilium de Sancto,
R. Et de Sion tuere eam.
V. Fiat pax in virtute Tua.
R. Et abundantia in turribus tuis.
V. Domine, exaudi orationem meam,
R. Et clamor meus ad Te veniat.
V. Dominus vobiscum.
R. Et cum spiritu tuo.

OREMUS

Omnipotens sempiterne Deus, aedificator et custos Ierusalem civitatis supernae, custodi die noctuque Rempublicam nostram cum habitatoribus eius, ut sit in eis domicilium incolumitatis et pacis.

Praetende, Domine, famulo tuo N. Praesidi Reipublicae dexteram coelestis auxilii, ut Te toto corde perquirat et quae digne postulat assequi mereatur. Per Christum Dominum nostrum. Amen.

Divinum auxilium maneat semper nobiscum. Amen."

—*TK* (official part), IV (1928), 16.

[22] *TK* (official part), IV (1928), 16.

A. Oottaviani ("Concordatum Lithuanicum"—*Apollinaris,* I [1928], p. 46) makes an interesting observation in the case where the President would not be a Catholic: "Iamvero posset dari casus in quo electus Praeses Reipublicae sit religionis non catholicae . . . Quaeri igitur posset utrum in hoc casu difficultas esset quoad executionem art. VIII Concordati circa preces liturgicas pro Praesidis prosperitate fundendas. Profecto exinde nullam oriri difficultatem iam erui potest ex iure concordatario praeexistente: S. Sedes enim in art. XI concordati initi anno 1886 cum Principatu Montisnigri, et in art. XVI concordati initi anno 1914 cum Regno Serbiae. consensit ut preces liturgicae pro Principe vel Rege iuxta notam formulam, *Domine salvum fac regem* etc.! fundentur, licet ageretur de dynastiis acatholicis.

Ratio est quia in casu catholici non communicant *in sacris,* et ceterum adimplent officio exorandi pro eis qui in sublimitate sunt iuxta monita apostolica, nulla exceptione facta aut distinctione inter catholicos et acatholicos, aut etiam infideles, ut ipsa antiqua praxis et patrum doctrina docet."

3. The Native Language.

After World War I there arose the important national question which involved the assurance of the rights of minorities. It had repercussions in the Lithuanian Concordat. Article XXII states:

> The Ordinaries shall attend to it that all the faithful will have religious assistance in their mother language according to the laws of the Church.[23]

The "religious assistance" refers to confessions, sermons, marriages, baptisms, devotions as permitted by the liturgy, and other acts of the Church.[24] This norm of the agreement guarantees the right to their native language not only for Lithuanians, but also for other nationalities in that country.[25]

The right to one's native language is a principle of the natural law and has found acceptance in the common public law.[26] The Church, at least since the IV Lateran Council (1215)[27] has had norms whereby Bishops in places where there is a population of various nationalities, were encouraged to have priests who would

The Lithuanian Constitution favors the policy that a member of the Church be elected as President. This is evident from section 65, which requires that the new President take an oath in the name of God (the text of the oath is given in the Constitution). The Constitution does not have a provision for a solemn promise. as it does for Ministers of State when they are not members of a Church (cf. section 98 of the Constitution).

[23] "Les Ordinaires veilleront à ce que tous les fidèles aient l'assistance religieus dans leur langue maternelle, selon les règles de l'Eglise."—*AAS*, XIX (1927), 431; A. Perugini, *Concordata vigentia*, p. 68.

[24] P. Malakauskis, *Viešosios Bažnytinės Teisės*, *p*. 163.

[25] Cf. P. Malakauskis, *Viešosios Bažnytinės Teisės*, p. 163.

[26] Cf. P. Parsy, *Les Concordats Récents, 1914-1935* (Rodez: G. Subervie [1936], pp. 242-243.

[27] J. Wright, *National Patriotism in Papal Teaching* (Westminster, Md.: Newman Bookshop, 1943), p. 145.

J. Eppstein, *The Catholic Tradition of the Law of Nations* (Washington: Catholic Association for International Peace, 1935), p. 387.

give religious assistance according to the diversities of rites and speech.[28]

The desire to bring religious assistance in the people's native language is one of the reasons that the Code in certain circumstances permits Ordinaries to seek apostolic approval for the creation of national parishes,[29] and that the Church is so anxious to have a native clergy in mission countries.[30]

The rights of the Lithuanian language are guaranteed by the Lithuanian Constitution, section 7:

> The official language shall be Lithuanian. The law shall provide in what districts of Lithuania and in what public institutions other languages may be used in addition to Lithuanian.[31]

For the religious assistance of the Church, the law concerning the language to be used is to be found in article XI of the Concordat.

[28] Decreta Generalis Concilii Lateranensis IV, Cap. IX. *De Diversis Ritibus in Eadem Fide:*

"Quoniam in plerisque partibus intra eamdem civitatem atque dioecesim permixti sunt populi diversarum linguarum, habentes sub una fide varios ritus et mores: districte praecipimus. ut pontifices hujusmodi civitatum sive dioecesum provideant viros idoneos, qui secundum diversitates rituum et linguarum Divina officia illis celebrent, et ecclesiastica sacramenta ministrent, instruendo eos verbo pariter et exemplo . . . Si propter praedictas causas urgens necessitas postulaverit, pontifex loci catholicum praesulem nationibus illis conformem provida deliberatione constituat sibi vicarium in praedictis . . . "—J. Harduin, *Acta Conciliorum et Epistolae Decretales, ac Constitutiones Summorum Pontificum* (12 vols., Parisiis: Typographia Regia, 1714-1715), VII. col. 27. This decree is incorporated in the *Corpus Iuris Canonici* in the Decretals of Gregory IX. Cf. c. 14, X, *de officio iudicis ordinarii,* I, 31. H. J. Schroeder (*Disciplinary Decrees of the General Councils, Text, Translation and Commentary* [St. Louis, Mo.: B. Herder Book Co.. 1937], pp. 250-251) offers an English translation and a short commentary.

[29] Can. 216, §4.

[30] Pius XI, Encyclical *Rerum Ecclesiae,* February 28, 1926—*AAS,* XVII (1926), 74, 76; cf. Pius XI, Apostolic Constitution *Ad Christianum Nomen,* April 8. 1935—*AAS,* XXVIII (1936), 94.

[31] "Valstybės kalba — lietuvių kalba. Įstatymu nustatoma kuriuose Lietuvos kraštuose ir kuriose viešose įstaigose, be lietuvių kalbos, gali būti vartojamos ir kitos kalbos."—*VŽ,* No. 608 (1938), 237.

which admits the right to the native language.[32] The right of the minorities to their own language was assured by the Declaration on the Protection of Minorities made by Lithuania, May 12, 1922, at the time of her admission to the League of Nations.[33]

[32] Cf. section 33 of the Lithuanian Constitution.—*VŽ,* No. 608 (1938), 238.

[33] M. O. Hudson, *International Legislation.* A Collection of the Texts of Multipartite International Instruments of General Interest (7 vols. covering 1919-1937; further volumes in preparation. Washington: Carnegie Endowment for International Peace, 1931-), II, 868-872.

Chapter XIII

SCHOOLS

1. Public Schools.

Pope Pius XI, who always manifested great interest in the Christian education of youth,[1] found ways to safeguard the rights of the Church in this field whenever there was occasion for concluding an agreement. Ann example of this is found in article XIII of the Lithuanian Concordat:

> 1. In all public schools and in all schools which receive state assistance religious instruction is obligatory. The competent Religious Authorities shall decide its programme and select the text-books. The nomination of teachers and the supervision of religious instruction, in that which concerns its content and the moral character of its teachers, shall be carried out in accordance with Canon Law. In case the Ordinary will deprive a teacher of the authorization which had been given him by the Ordinary, the teacher shall *ipso facto* be deprived of his right to teach religion.[2]

These provisions are in accord with the norms of the Code, as expressed in canons 1372, 1373 and 1381.[3]

[1] Cf. Encyclical *Rappresantanti in Terra* on the Christian Education of Youth, December 31, 1929—*AAS*, XXI (1929), 730-753.

[2] "Dans toutes les écoles publiques, ou subventionnées par l'Etat, l'enseignement religieux est obligatoire. L'autorité religieuse compétente en établira le programme et choisira les textes. La nomination des enseignants et la surveillance de l'enseignement religieux, en ce qui concerne son contenue et la morale des enseignants, s'effectuera conformément au Droit Canon. Au cas où l'Ordinaire retirerait à un enseignant l'autorisation qui'l lui avait donnée, ce dernier sera par là même privé du droit d'enseigner la Religion."—*AAS*, XIX (1927), 428-429; A. Perugini, *Concordata vigentia*, p. 64.

[3] Article XIII agrees also with the local ecclesiastical legislation: the Ordinary of the diocese of Samogitia, after previous understanding with the Ministry of Education, in 1923 published (in *Ganytojas*, No. 12 [1923]

The Lithuanian Constitution also provides for obligatory instruction in religion even in the public schools:

> Section 41. Religious instruction shall be given in the elementary and secondary schools to those pupils who belong to the churches or other confessional organizations which are recognized by the State. The cases in which religious instruction may be given in other schools shall be defined by law.[4]

The law concerning the teachers of religion in secondary schools, published on April 7, 1927, is in conformity with the Concordat.[5]

Later legislation tended to stress the right of the Ministry of Education to appoint and dismiss teachers of religion. However, the text of these laws admitted that only persons having permis-

263) the following instructions: "Vyskupas skiria tikybos dėstytojus ir paskyrimo raštus siunčia tikybos moktojams kunigams betarpiai, pranešdamas sykiu apie įvykusį paskyrimą Pradžios Mokslo Departamentui; turintiems teisės tikybos dėstyti nekunigams (mokytojams ar kitiems pasauliniems asmenims) paskyrimo raštas siunčiamas per Pradžios Mokslo Departamentą.

Kunigai dekanai, lankydami savo dekanatus, turi teisės ir pareigos tikrinti, kaip tikyba dėstoma pradžios mokylose . . . Religijos mokymas visose, esančiose parapijos ribose pradžios mokylose yra tiesioginė vietinio klebono ir jo kunigų vikarų pareiga, kaipo dvasiškųjų ganytojų, einant 1329 ir 1373, § 1 kanonų normomis. Iš tos priežasties vietos parapijos kunigai yra kanonų atžvilgiu laikomi sykiu ir pradžios mokyklų kapelionais bei mokyklų dėstytojais . . .

Jei vietiniai kunigai negali dėl svarbios priežasties patys asmeniškai lankyti kurios mokyklos, tenai tikybos mokymas gali būti pavestas vietos mokytojui, jei jis atsako religijos mokytojo ypatybėms, ar kitam pasauliniam asmeniui, žiūrint Kanonų Teisės Kodekso nurodymų *de missione canonica*."—Cited from *TK*, IV (1928), 3-4.

[4] "Pradinėse ir vidurinėse mokyklose tikyba dėstoma mokiniams priklausantiems prie Valstybės pripažintų bažnyčių ir kitų tolygių tikybinių organizacijų. Kuriose kitose mokyklose tikyba dėstoma-nustatoma įstatymu." —*VŽ*, No. 608 (1938), 239.

[5] "Atskirų dalykų vidurinėje ir aukštesnėje mokykloje turi teisės mokyti—1. Tikybos—a) dvasininkai ir b) asmens, kurie turi mokytojui reikalingą mokslo cenzą ir atatinkamos tikybinės organizacijos leidimą."—*VŽ*, No. 248 (1927), 2.

sion for that purpose from the ecclesiastical authorities could be appointed.[6]

The circulars of the officials of the Ministry of Education concerning the elementary schools show the favorable attitude of the State towards religious instruction. The principals of the schools were reminded that in their institutions an atmosphere of respect for the religion of the parents should prevail.[7]

The inspectors of the primary schools were informed that Catholic priests did not need permission from the civil authorities to teach religion.[8] Then, too, the principals of the elementary public schools were instructed to permit priests to have their classes of religion at any time they should arrive, and to take into account the fact that frequently their duties prevented them from regular

[6] "Pradžios mokyklų įstatymas. § 11. Pradžios mokykloje einami šie dalykai: 1/tikyba . . . § 43. Tikybai dėstyti pradžios mokykloje Švietimo Ministerija skiria dvasininkus ir nedvasininkus, turinčius atitinkamos dvasinės vyresnybės leidimą."—*VŽ*, No. 541 (1936), 1-3.

"Vidurinių mokyklų įstatymas. § 14. Vidurinėje mokykloje einami šie dalykai: 1/tikyba . . . § 33. Tikybos mokytojus pasirenka ir skiria Švietimo Ministeris iš tų, kas turi atitinkamos dvasinės vyresnybės leidimą."—*VŽ*, No. 541 (1936), 5-6.

[7] The Circular of the Director of the First Department, January 30, 1931, No. 261: "Atsižiūrėdamas į pradžios mokyklų įstatymo reikalavimą, kad visos prodžios mokyklos būtų vedamos valstybingumo ir tėvų konfesijos dvasioje (§3) ir į tai, kad už visą mokyklos darbą atsako jos vedėjai (Pradžios mokyklų įstatymo pakeitimo §21), prašau p.p. Inspektorius paskelbti mokyklų vedėjams ir patiems, lankant mokyklas, prižiūrėti, kad sakytasis įstatymo reikalavimas būtų visu rimtumu ir atsidėjus vykdomas ir pasireikštų tuo, kad pradžios mokyklos mokiniai būtų auklėjami didžiai branginti ir gerbti savo valstybę, tautą ir jos vyriausybę, branginti savus ir lygiai gerbti kitų žmonių įsitikinimus. Pas. Švietimo Ministeris K. Šakenis, I-jo Departamento Direktorius J. Vokietaitis."*ŠMŽ*, No. 1 (1931), 69-70.

[8] The Circular of the Director of the First Department, November 24, 1931, No. 24177: "Pranešu, kad Departamento š.m. raštas Nr. 22990, kuriame įsakoma prad. mokyklų vedėjams neleisti asmenims be Švietimo Ministerijos leidimo dėstyti tikybą prad. mokyklose, katalikų kunigų neliečia. Pas. Direktorius Miškinis."—*ŠMŽ*, No. 10 (1931), 44.

attendance at schools.[9] The respect shown towards religion in the public schools of Lithuania was highly lauded even in foreign countries.[10]

2. The Faculty of Theology and Philosophy in the State University.

At the time that the Concordat was concluded there was in Lithuania only one University, the State University of Kaunas.[11] This University, from the day of its foundation, February 16, 1922, had a Faculty of Theology and Philosophy which was under the supervision of the Church.[12]

[9] The Circular of the Minister of Education, March 8, 1930, No. 231: "Prad. mokyklų inspektoriams. Švietimo Ministerijoje gauta žinių, kad kaikurie Inspektoriai reikalauja iš tikybos mokytojų kunigų būtinai atvykti į pamokas nustatytomis dienomis ir valandomis. Kunigai, ypač gyveną toliau nuo mokyklų, dėl savo pareigų parapijose nevisuomet gali nustatytą valandą atvykti į pamokas. Todėl įsakau p.p. Inspektoriams paaiškinti mokyklų vedėjams, kad jie nekliudytų tikybos mokytojams kunigams, negalintiems dėl savo tiesioginių pareigų nustatytu laiku atvykti į mokyklas, atlikti tikybos pamokų kitomis valandomis. Tuo reikalu tikybos mokytojai kunigai turi susitarti su mokyklų vedėjais, kad nebūtų trukdomas mokymo darbas mokyklose. Inž. K. Šakenis, Švietimo Ministeris." —*Švietimo Darbas* (The Work of Education; official part), No. 3 (1930), 144.

[10] E.g.: "Ne abbiamo un esempio nel recentissimo Concordato tra la Santa Sede e la Lithuania. Quanto ivi riguarda la scuola e l'insegnamento publico è bene che sia conosciuto in Italia, affinchè i cattolici sappiano quello che è di loro stretto e imprescindibile diritto in una nazione totalmente cattolica, e coloro che li rimproverano di esorbitanti pretensioni abbiano una conveniente risposta e una efficace confutazione ai loro sofismi."—*La Civiltà Cattolica,* anno LXXIX (1928), tom. II, 24.

[11] There were other institutions of higher education, such as the Academy of Agriculture, the Conservatory of Music, etc. Cf. E. Harrison, *Lithuania,* pp. 92-102.

[12] Cf. *Lietuvos Universitetas. The University of Lithuania* (publication of the University on the fifth anniversary; Kaunas: Valstybės Spaustuvė, 1927), pp. 36-38, 147-152.

Cf. Statutes of the University, section 5.—A. Merkys, *Lietuvos Įstatymai,* p. 966.

The Concordat guaranteed the rights of the Church concerning the choice of the personnel of the Faculty. The same provisions of article XIII which applied to teachers of religion in the public schools [13] had effect here:

> The same principles governing the choice and revocation of the teachers shall be applied to the professors, associate professors and assistants in the Faculty of Theology and Philosophy, which the State maintains at its expense.[14]

The State by this norm not only admitted the obligation to provide the Faculty with the necessary subsidies, but also accepted the right of the Church to choose the professors and other members of the staff; and this is in agreement with the rule of canon 1381, § 3. However, in practice, the condition of the Faculty of Theology and Philosophy depended upon the changes in policy of the Lithuanian Government and the choice of the Minister of Education.[15]

The Faculty and also its power to confer degrees was approved by the Holy See,[16] but the State for some years did not recognize the diplomas of the Philosophical section. The recognition was granted on January 9, 1939, having retroactive effect.[17]

[13] See the text of the Concordat in the previous section.

[14] The writer's translation. Original text in article XIII: "Les mêmes principes, concernant le choix et la révocation des enseignants seront appliqués aux professeurs, aux agrégés et aux adjoints universitaires de la Faculté de Philosophie et Théologie, que l'Etat maintient à ses frais."—*AAS,* XIX (1927), 429; A. Perugini, *Concordata vigentia,* p. 64.

[15] The Nationalists, who controlled the Government from December 17, 1926, and who were in a minority in the country were suspicious that the Faculty of Theology and Philosophy might form the leaders of the Christian Democrats. This party had been disbanded, but it still had strong roots in the people.

[16] Decretum Sacrae Congregationis de Seminariis et Studiorum Universitatibus, June 15, 1928.—*TK* (official part), IV (1928), 125-126.

[17] The Law of Recognition of the Diplomas: "Buvusieji Vyt. Didžiojo Universiteto Teologijos-Filisofijos Fakulteto klausytojai, kurie nuo 1930 m. birželio 7 d. iki 1937 m. lapkričio 17 d. gavo diplomus su pažymėjimu, kad baigė filosofijos skyrių, laikomi nuo diplomo gavimo dienos turinčiais aukštojo mokslo baigimo teises."—*VŽ,* No. 631 (1939), 7.

By the law of August 14, 1931,[18] the number of Chairs in the Faculty had been reduced from 22 to 17.[19]

The first statutes of the University (1922) conceded that the choice of the professors of the Faculty should take place according to Canon Law.[20] Later, in 1927, this principle was included in the Concordat. The civil law, too, on August 14, 1931, allowed that the personnel of the Faculty be appointed according to the norms of article XIII of the Concordat.[21] However, the new statutes of the University, drawn up in 1937, do not reproduce these norms. There are provisions which, contrary to the requirements of article XIII, emphasize the power of the President and of the Minister of Education in the choice of the teaching personnel of the University.[22]

Article XXVI of the Concordat states that all laws contrary to the Concordat shall be void.[23] This brings hope that in the Faculty of Theology and Philosophy, instead of the general provisions of the latest statutes of the University, the special norms of the artice XIII of the Concordat will be applied.

[18] *VŽ,* No. 363 (1931), 1.

[19] *Vytauto Didžiojo Universitetas* (The University of Vytautas the Great; Kaunas: V. D. Universiteto Kanceliarija, 1933), p. 189.

[20] "Teologijos-Filosofijos Fakultetas renkasi profesorius prisilaikydamas kanonų teisės."—A. Merkys, *Lietuvos Įstatymai,* p. 966.

[21] The Law concerning the changes of the Statutes of the University. "Teologijos-Filosofijos fakulteto personalas parenkamas ir skiriamas Vytauto Didžiojo Universiteto Statuto (20 str.) ir Šv. Sosto ir Lietuvos Respublikos konkordato XIII str. nustatyta tvarka."—*VŽ,* No. 363 (1931), 1.

[22] "§48. Vyresniojo mokslo personalo kandidatus renka fakulteto taryba. Skiria juos Respublikos Prezidentas.

Privatdocentų ir jaunesniojo mokslo personalo kandidatus renka fakulteto taryba. Tvirtina juos Švietimo Ministeris."—*VŽ,* No. 591 (1937). 366.

[23] "Toutes lois, ordonnances ou décrets, qui seraient en contradiction avec les stipulations des articles précédents, seront de ce fait même annulés, dès entrée en vigueur du présent Concordat."—*AAS,* XIX (1927), 433; A. Perugini, *Concordata vigentia,* p. 69.

3. Seminaries.

All restrictions regarding seminaries which existed in Lithuania before World War I as a result of former agreements with Russia [24] were abolished by article XIII, 2°, of the Concordat:

> In all dioceses, the Catholic Church shall possess in accordance with Canon Law Ecclesiastical Seminaries aided by the State, which She shall direct and whose professors She shall nominate.
>
> The certificates of studies issued by the major Seminaries shall suffice for teaching religion in all public schools and in all schools which receive state assistance.[25]

This norm is in conformity with the provisions of canons 1352, 1354 and 1357.

The Lithuanian Constitution, section 28, guarantees the liberty of Church to conduct seminaries:

> The Churches and other confessional organizations which are recognized by the State shall be allowed freely to . . . own institutions designed to train for ecclesiastical duties.[26]

When the minor seminary of the diocese of Telšiai was established, the President of the State promulgated its statutes. These are in agreement with article XIII of the Concordat; they recog-

[24] Concordat of 1847, section 22.—A. Mercati, *Raccolta di Concordati*, p. 758; agreement of 1882, section B.—A. Mercati, *Op. cit.*, p. 1016-1017; convention of 1907, sections I-IV.—A. Mercati, *Op cit.*, 1097-1098.

[25] "Dans tous les diocèses, l'Eglise catholique en conformité avec le Droit Canon possédera des Séminaires ecclésiastiques subventionnés par l'Etat, qu'Elle dirigera et dont Elle nommera les enseignants.

Les brevets d'études délivrés par les grands Séminaires seront suffisants pour enseigner la Religion dans toutes les écoles publiques ou subventionées par l'Etat."—*AAS*, XIX (1927). 429; A. Perugini, *Concordata vigentia*, p. 64.

[26] "Valstybės pripažintos bažnyčios bei kitos tolygios tikybinės organizacijos gali laisvai . . . laikyti dvasines mokyklas dvasininkams ruošti." —*VŽ*, No. 608 (1938), 238.

nize the right of the Bishop to found the seminary, to designate the program of disciplines in religion, philosophy and Church chant, and to appoint the rector, spiritual director and the professors. The diplomas of the seminary are recognized as sufficient to admit the student to the State University. The representatives of the Ministry of Education, however, were allowed to visit classes of general instruction (as, e.g., classes in the Lithuanian Language, History, etc.).[27]

The civil law granted to the graduates of major seminaries (to priests) the right to teach religion in elementary and secondary schools.[28] The seminaries received subsidies from the State.[29]

4. Christian Education.

One of the greatest aims of the Church is to give her children a true Christian education and to protect them from the dangers of lay or neutral schools.[30]

The Lithuanian Concordat is an example of the realization of that aim. Article XIII, 3°-4° states:

> In all public schools and in all schools which receive State assistance, the State shall co-operate with the Ordinaries in affording to all students proper facilities for the due performance of their religious duties.
>
> In matters which concern the education of Catholic youth, the State acknowledges in all Ordinaries the rights accorded them by Canon 1381, and shall attach importance to their justifiable complaints.[31]

[27] *VŽ,* No. 332 (1930), 5-6. Cf. *VŽ,* No. 529 (1936), 2-3.

[28] *VŽ,* No. 248 (1927), 2; *VŽ,* No. 541 (1936), 3.

[29] *VŽ,* No. 701 (1940), 280.

[30] Cf. can. 1372, 1374.

[31] "Dans toutes les écoles publiques ou subventionnées par l'Etat celuici veillera d'accord avec les Ordinaires à ce que les élèves puissent convenablement accomplir leurs devoirs religieux.

This provision of the Concordat is entirely in conformity with the Code. It explicitly accepts the norm of canon 1381, which thus becomes the norm endorsed and confirmed by the agreement. Canon 1381 declares that religious instruction in all schools is subject to the authority and inspection of the Church; the Ordinaries have the right and duty to see that in the schools of their territory nothing be taught or done contrary to faith and good morals. Moreover, the Ordinaries have the right to approve the teachers of religion and the manuals, or to demand that, in the interest of religion and morals, specific teachers and books be removed.[32]

The provision implicitly includes the right of the Ordinaries to visit the schools, as is expressed in canon 1382.[33] By this norm of article XIII, the rights of the Church are recognized not only in the elementary and secondary schools, but even in institutions of higher education. This is clear from the fact that the Lithuanian Concordat does not contain any restriction such as is found in the norm of the Polish Concordat concerning this matter.[34]

En ce qui concerne l'éducation de la jeunesse catholique l'Etat reconnait aux Ordinaires les droits prévus par le canon 1381 et il donnera suite aux remontrances justifiées des mêmes Ordinaires."—*AAS*, XIX (1927), 429; A. Perugini, *Concordata vigentia*, p. 64.

[32] Can. 1381, § 1. Religiosa iuventutis institutio in scholis quibuslibet auctoritati et inspectioni Ecclesiae subiicitur.

§2. Ordinariis locorum ius et officium est vigilandi ne in quibusvis scholis sui territorii quidquam contra fidem vel bonos mores tradatur aut fiat.

§3. Eisdem similiter ius est approbandi religionis magistros et libros; itemque, religionis morumque causa. exigendi ut tum magistri tum libri removeantur."

[33] Cf. R. Ruzé, "A propos des Nouveaux Accords du Saint-Siege: Concordat avec la Lithuanie, Modus Vivendi avec la Tchecoslovaquie"—*Revue de Droit International et de Legislation Comparée*, X (1929), 362.

[34] Article XIII of the Polish Concordat: "Dans toutes les écoles publiques, à l'exception des écoles supérieures . . . "—*AAS*, XVII (1925), 277; A. Perugini, *Concordata vigentia*, p. 39. Cf. A. Malakauskis, *Viešosios Bažnytinės Teisės*, p. 159.

The provision of the Concordat concerning the freedom of the students in the performance of their religious duties receives confirmation in section 20 of the Lithuanian Constitution:

> The State shall guard the citizens' freedom of conscience . . . If they are in the employ of any person, members of all religious denominations shall be granted the time required for the performance of their religious duties.[35]

The provisions of the Concordat regarding the Christian education of youth were highly praised in other countries.[36] In Lithuania, however, Christian education encountered some difficulties, especially in the case of Catholic associations. This point will be treated in the next chapter with reference to Catholic Action.

5. Private Schools.

Pope Pius XI paid great attention to private schools.[37]

This aim of His Holiness likewise found a guarantee in article XIII, 5°, of the Concordat:

> All schools which are under the supervision of the Ordinary and conform to the program of the Ministry of Public Instruction are to be on an equal basis with State schools as regards the value of their diplomas.[38]

[35] "Valstybė saugo piliečio sąžinės laisvę . . . Tikintiesiems, kurie yra kieno nors valdžioje, duodama laiko savo tikybos pareigoms atlikti."—*VŽ*, No. 608 (1938), 238.

[36] E.g.: "Optimae sunt dispositiones art. XIII de scholis et seminariis, nunquam satis laudandae, cum doctrinam catholicam in Codice concinne accurateque traditam (can. 1352 ss., 1372 ss.) referant."—F. Cappello, "De Natura Concordatorum"—*JP*, VIII (1928), 17.

[37] "Igitur, vix invenire est Concordatum in quo Pius XI praetermiserit cautiones exigere de scholis deque recta iuvenum institutione: et intelligitur quantum eaedem conferent ad bonum sociale nationum."—A. Ottaviani, "Jus Concordatum Pii XI"—*Apollinaris*, II (1929), 287.

[38] The writer's translation. Original text: "Toutes les écoles qui se trouvent sous la dépendance de l'Ordinaire et se conforment au programme du Ministère de l'Instruction publique sont assimilées, pour ce qui regarde la valeur des diplômes, aux Ecoles de l'Etat."—*AAS*, XIX (1927). 429; A. Perugini, *Concordata vigentia*, p. 65.

By this norm the State indirectly recognizes the right of the Church to have private schools, which is a principle rooted in the natural law,[39] in full conformity with the doctrine of canon 1375.

The Lithuanian Constitution, in section 39, likewise has a provision which assures the Church the right to conduct her schools:

> Citizens, as individuals and as members of associations, as well as churches or other confessional organizations, shall be authorized to conduct educational institutions in accordance with the conditions and provisions laid down by law.[40]

The civil laws, in addition, have prpovisions from which follows the right of the Church to conduct seminaries for teachers,[41] special schools of agriculture,[42] schools of handicraft and trade,[43] and other schools.[44]

In many cases, the State recognized the right of private Catholic schools to issue diplomas, and attributed the same worth to these diplomas as the State itself did to those issued by the public schools.[45] There was, however, a tendency on the part of the

[39] Cf. The Decision of the U. S. Supreme Court in the Oregon School Case, June 1, 1925: "The fundamental theory of liberty upon which all governments in this Union repose excludes any general power of the State to standardize its children by forcing them to accept instruction from public teachers only. The child is not the mere creature of the State; those who nurture him and direct his destiny have the right coupled with the high duty, to recognize and prepare him for additional obligations."—*Oregon School Cases.* Complete Record (Baltimore; The Belvedere Press, Inc., [1925]), p. 942.

Pope Pius XI cited this quotation in his Encyclical *Rappresentanti in Terra,* December 31, 1929.—*AAS,* XXI (1929), 735-736.

[40] "Atskiriems piliečiams ir organizacijoms, taip pat bažnyčioms bei kitoms tolygioms tikybinėms organizacijoms, leidžiama įstatymu nustatytomis sąlygomis ir tvarka laikyti auklėjamąsias įstaigas ir mokyklas." —*VŽ,* No. 608 (1938), 239.

[41] *VŽ,* No. 361 (1931), 1-5; *VŽ,* No. 693 (1940), 86.

[42] *VŽ,* No. 226 (1926), 1.

[43] *VŽ,* No. 308 (1929), 2.

[44] *VŽ,* No. 592 (1937), 375.

[45] Cf. *VŽ,* No. 255 (1927), 3; *VŽ,* No. 247 (1927), 5; *VŽ,* No. 419 (1933), 27.

Government to restrain the freedom and the rights of Catholic private schools: the legal position of a number of them was changed many times,[46] several of them were transformed into State schools,[47] and some Catholic institutions of education were dissolved.[48] When Catholics had decided to found a Catholic University in Lithuania and had made certain initial preparations, the functioning of that institution was hindered by the prohibition of the Nationalist Government. As a consequence, such a university was actually never realized.[49] Such acts of the Government were contrary to the stipulations of the Concordat.[50]

[46] For example, the gymnasium *Pavasaris* in Kaunas. Cf. *VŽ*, No. 248 (1927), 5 and *VŽ*, No. 652 (1937), 432.

[47] For example, the gymnasium of *Saulė* in Utena.

[48] This was the lot of the three Catholic seminaries for teachers: *Simano Daukanto, Saulės* and *L. K. M. Kultūros dr-jos,* all three in Kaunas.

[49] The Catholic University of Lithuania was approved by the Holy See June 18, 1932. It was formally founded by an act of the Bishops of Lithuania, August 5, 1932, but it never had a chance to function.—*TK* (official part), VIII (1932), 69.; J. Eretas, *Suvažiavimo Darbai* 1933 (Acts of the Convention of the Catholic Academy of Science; Kaunas: Liet. Kat. Mokslo Akademija, 1935), pp. 257-258, footnote 1.

[50] This was a hard blow to the hopes which Pope Pius XI had expressed June 24, 1928, in the Letter *Ad RR.PP.DD. Josephum Skvireckas Archiepiscopum Kaunensem, ceterosque Lithuaniae Episcopos,* issued on the occasion of the visit of the Lithuanian Bishops to the Holy See: "Principio, laetamur equidem magnae vobis curae esse ut recte iuvenes educentur: quam quidem ad rem assequendam, cum necesse sit ut tria illa societatis humanae fundamenta, familia scilicet religio, civitas, mutua opera conspirent, tum patet praecipuum id esse ecclesiasticae autoritatis munus, penes quam rationes ipsae nituntur rectae honestaeque vitae, fides nempe ac pietas. Quare libenter propositum vestrum laudamus ea promovendi instituta, scholas imprimis atque collegia, ubi et christianis principiis iuvenum mentes imbuuntur, et ipsorum animi bonis moribus conformantur. . . . Nos ceterum, ut aliis rebus iisdemque gravibus, ita iuvenili eiusmodi institutioni per pacta illa conventa opportune perspeximus quae feliciter Apostolicam Sedem inter et Lithuaniam recens inita sunt: ac fore confidimus conventa ipsa sancte inviolateque servata eam fructuum copiam in hoc etiam rerum genere allaturam, quam in optatis habemus, quaeque ab Ecclesia sperari licet cum vim suam inter populos exercere libera potest."—*AAS,* XX (1928), 254-255.

Chapter XIV

CATHOLIC ACTION

The great promoter of Catholic Action, Pope Pius XI, already in his first Encyclical *Ubi Arcano Dei,* December 23, 1922, stated that Catholic Action was one of his most cherished ideas.[1] His Holiness, Pope Pius XI, wanted to provide the necessary legal basis for the development of Catholic Action in each country. The first great success in this regard during the era of Concordats of Pope Pius XI is to be found in the Lithuanian Concordat, for article XXV guaranteed by treaty the freedom of Catholic Action:

> The State will grant full liberty of organization and action to associations the object of which is principally religious, and which form part of the *Action Catholique,* and, as such, are subject to the authority of the Bishops.[2]

By this stipulation there is admitted 1) full freedom to establish and to organize associations for Catholic Action; and 2) full freedom of action for these associations.

To enjoy the privilege of full liberty, it is necessary that associations have the following qualities:

1. Their principal purpose must be religious, although this does not exclude their secondary ends, such as, culture, economics, and education (science, theatre, athletics, etc.)[3]

[1] "Huc denique pertinet omnium eorum summa, seu complexio, institutorum, consiliorum, et operum quae *nominae actionis catholicae,* nobis carissimae perhibentur."—*AAS,* XIV (1922), 693.

[2] "L'Etat accordera pleine liberté d'organisation et de fontionnement aux associations poursuivant des buts principalement religieux, faisant partie de *l'Action Catholique* et. comme telles, dépendant de l'Autorité de l'Ordinaire."—*AAS,* XIX (1927), 432; A. Perugini, *Concordata vigentia,* p. 69.

[3] A. Ottaviani, *Compendium Iuris Publici Ecclesiastici* (Typis Polyglotis Vaticanis, 1936), n. 292; A. Cicognani, *Canon Law,* p. 474.

2. These societies must be affiliated with the Center of Catholic Action; in the case of Lithuania, they must be members of the *Katalikų Veikimo Centras.*[4]

3. The association must be subject to the authority of the Ordinary.[5]

Keeping principally the religious end in view, the associations pertaining to Catholic Action must, however, abstain from the activities of political parties.[6]

The provision of article XXV of the Concordat is in agreement with the norms of the Code of Canon Law as stated in canons 684, 686, 687, 689, and 691; it is also in harmony with the statements of the Holy See.[7]

[4] This is the leading, central organ of Catholic Action in Lithuania, as is stated in the pastoral letter of the Bishops of the country, February 1, 1928: "Katalikiškoms draugijoms vadovauti įsteigta yra Katalikų Veikimo Centras. Žinote ir patys, kaip dabartinis Šventasis Tėvas Pijus XI aukštai įvertina katalikiškąją akciją, kaip jąja rūpinasi, kad ji visur katalikuose klestėtų; net mūsų Konkordate jos veikimo laisvė yra garantuota."—*TK* (official part), IV (1928), 28.

[5] Cf. P. Malakauskis, *Viešosios Bažnytinės Teisės,* p. 165.

[6] Pope Pius XI in his letter *Ad RR.PP.DD. Josephum Skvireckas Archiepiscopum Kaunensem, ceterosque Lithuaniae Episcopos,* June 24, 1928, states: "Permagni sane ad communem salutem interest, quemadmodum patet, ut actio huiusmodi — quae quidem ab omnibus ex eadem natione catholicis, cum omnibus prosit, promoveri debet — ne, politicis rebus implicata, intra angustos alicuius factionis fines coerceatur. Etenim seponantur oportet factionum commoda cum de religionis rebus agatur, per quas maximae et verae civitati ipsi utilitates afferuntur. Cumque *actio catholica* nihil sit aliud nisi *actio religiosa,* non eadem studiis partium, sed plena catholicorum concordia niti ac consistere debet eo conspirantium ut communis christianae vitae sensus atque usus privatum publicae retineantur. . . . At praesertim cleri est actionem catholicam a politicis rebus seiungere; cum enim religiosas res populi universi is curare debeat, prorsus dedecet factioni alicui studere; siquidem cavendum est ne ministerii eius dignitas inter partium conflictus deteratur neve qui ad contrarias factiones pertinent, errore fortasse decepti, a religione abalienentur."—*AAS,* XX (1928), 256-257.

[7] Pope Pius XI in Letter *Quamvis Nostra,* October 27, 1935, exhorts the hierarchy "ut hoc firmum validumque Actionis Catholicae adiumentum

The freedom of the associations which belong to Catholic Action follows directly from the freedom in the exercise of social activities and the freedom of association, as guaranteed by the Lithuanian Constitution:

> Section 25. The State shall safeguard the freedom of its citizens in the exercise of their social activities, more particularly, freedom of the press, and of association and meeting, seeing to it that such activities shall not be detrimental to the State.[8]

The principles of Catholic Action were taught during the periods set apart for religious instruction even in the public schools of Lithuania.[9] The civil law of Lithuania admitted the possibility of exceptional rights for associations having a religious purpose.[10] However, when the Nationalistic Government of Lithuania made a more pronounced turn toward totalitarianism, the condition of Catholic Action in that country deteriorated considerably. The rights of associations were restricted. These restrictions concerned the founding of associations,[11] the age of their members,[12] and their functioning.[13] Students, except those in higher institutions of learning (universities and similar educa-

ad bonos mores in societate restituendos ubique constituatur, ita ut quam primum in omnibus diecesibus praeclara haec agmina cogantur e strenuis militibus, qui Dei Ecclesiaeque iura ac rationes fortiter tueantur et quocumque inducant 'sensum Christi,' qui et singulis et familiis et societati ipsi civili est prosperitatis pignus atque praesidium."—*AAS,* XXVIII (1936), 164.

[8] "Valstybė saugo piliečių visuomeninio veikimo laisvę, ypač spaudoje, draugijose ir susirinkimuose, žiūrėdama, kad jis nebūtų veikiamas kenksminga Valstybei kryptimi."—*VŽ,* No. 608 (1938), 238.

[9] Cf. The Program of Religious Instruction for Schools of Trade and Handicraft.—*ŠMŽ,* No. 3 (1938), 139.

[10] Cf. The Law of Associations, sections 64-65.—*VŽ,* No. 522 (1936), 1-4.

[11] The Law of Associations, section 7.—*VŽ,* No. 522 (1936), I.

[12] Members must be no younger than 18 years of age.—*VŽ,* No. 522 (1936), 2.

[13] For example, if there were less than 12 members, the association had to be dissolved.—*VŽ,* No. 522 (1936), 2.

tional units) were forbidden to be members of associations.[14]

By a special circular, issued on August 30, 1930 by the Minister of Education to the directors of secondary schools and of schools of professional education, all associations in these schools were closed, including the association of Catholic students (*Ateitininkai*). An exception was made only for Boy Scouts and Girl Scout groups, and for the Associations of the Red Cross.[15]

The decree of the Ministry of Education dissolving Catholic associations was contrary to the norms of the Concordat, as expressed in articles XIII and XXV, and hence was a source of confusion.[16]

[14] The Law of Associations, section 36.—*VŽ*, No. 522 (1936), 3.

[15] "Visų Švietimo Ministerijos žinioje esančių vidurinių, aukštesniųjų bendrojo lavinimo ir specialinių mokyklų direktoriams.

Mokymas ir auklėjimas privalo vieningos vadovybės. Tai yra valdžios pareiga ir teisė. Už jaunimo mokymą ir auklėjimą ji atsako prieš tėvus, prieš visuomenę ir prieš visą tautą. Dėl to Švietimo Ministerija, giliai įsitikinusi, kad moksleivių kuopelės yra žalingos mokymui ir auklėjimui, ryžosi padaryti galą jų atgyventai tradicijai.

Taigi, pasirėmus 'Vidurinių ir aukštesniųjų mokyklų įstatymo' § 61 (Vyr. Žin. Nr. 190, eil. 1289), nuo šių mokslo metų pradžios visos, be jokios išimties politiškai visuomeninio pobūdžio moksleivių organizacijos visose Lietuvos mokyklose (vidurinėse ir aukštesiosiose bendrojo lavinimo ir specialinėse) Švietimo Ministerijos nutarimu uždaromos, 'Instrukcijų pedagaginiam aukštesniųjų ir vidurinių mokyklų presonalui' I skyriaus 3 skiltis 'Apie mokinių organizacijas' (§§23-33) anuliuojama. Visų tų mokyklų p.p. direktoriams įsakau neatidėliojant uždaryti visas tokias moksleivių kuopeles ir apie jų uždarymą tuojau pranešti Švietimo Ministerijai.

Paliekama tėra tik skautų brolijos organizacija, kuri auklėja jaunimą taip, kaip mokyklos drausmė reikalauja, ir skatina lygiai visus savo narius rūpestingai mokytis. . . .

Jų [mokinių] auklėjimu tesirūpina tie, kurių tai yra pareiga ir teisė—tėvai ir mokykla."—*Švietimo Darbas* (official part), No. 9 (1930), 393-394; Cf. A. Ottaviani, *Compendium Iuris Publici Ecclesiastici,* n. 292.

[16] The Church remonstrated against this decree. The Catholic association of students (*Ateitininkai*) functioned under the protection of the Church, meeting in places other than the school, but its members were punished by the officials of the Ministry of Education. Especially difficult was the position of the chaplains of the schools.

Obligatory instruction in religion, however, remained in force.

Chapter XV

THE PROPERTY AND INCOME OF THE CHURCH AND OF ECCLESIASTICAL PERSONS

1. Recognition of the Right to the Property which the Church Possesses.

Russia, which had occupied Lithuania in 1795, confiscated in the nineteenth century the greater part of the property of the Catholic Church in that country.[1] Russia refused to restore this property even when the concordat was signed in 1847.[2]

After World War I, when Russia collapsed and Lithuania regained her independence, a great part of the property was returned to the possession of the Church. However, the legal ownership of the Church was not immediately recognized; according to civil law, all the goods which had been confiscated by the Russians, were now declared to be under the protection of the Lithuanian Government, until a final decision should be reached.[3]

The Concordat, in article XXII, 1°-2°, provided the final decision concerning the property which had already been returned to the possession of the Church:

[1] According to an estimate made by Russians, the property had a value of 110 million rubles (about 55 million dollars).—*TK,* IV (1928), 107.

[2] *Articoli non Concordati,* Section 9: "Le Plénipotentiaire de Sa Sainteté a insisté sur la restitution à faire au clergé de ses biens. Les Plénipotentiaires de S. M. ont déclaré qu'ils n'avaient aucune instruction spéciale sur cet objet. . . . "—A. Mercati, *Raccolta di Concordati,* p. 763.

[3] The Law Concerning the Confiscated Churches, the Land and other Property which had belonged to the Church, sections 1-2: "Įstatymas dėl rusų vyriausybės konfiskuotųjų bažnyčių, bažnytinių žemių ir kitokių turtų.

1. Visas bažnyčias ir vienuolynus, jų žemes, miškus, vandenis, namus, malūnus, kapitalus ir kitokius judomus ir nejudomus turtus, kurie įvairiais laikais buvo sekvestruoti, konfiskuoti arba atimti rusų vyriausybės, Lietuvos valstybė ima savo žinion ligi galutinai nusprendus jų likimą Steigiamajam Seimui.

2. Naudotis paminėtomis 1-me punkte bažnyčiomis ir jų turtais galima tik su Valstybės Vyriausybės Žinia."—*VŽ,* No. 11 (1919), 4.

1. The Republic of Lithuania recognizes the property rights of juridical persons, ecclesiastical and religious, to all movable and immovable goods, capital assets, rents and other titles which these juridical persons actually possess in the territory of the State.

2. The Republic of Lithuania agrees that, in cases wherein they should not yet be entered in the registers of *hypothèque* or of other equivalent juridical instruments in the names of juridical persons who possess them (Bishoprics, Chapters, Congregations, Religious Orders, Seminaries, parochial benefices and so forth), the above mentioned property rights be inscribed therein, and this upon a declaration of the competent Ordinary, certified by the competent civil authority.[4]

The Government recognized the ownership of real property, capital assets, rents and other rights of property which the Church possessed at the time the Concordat was concluded,[5] that is, on September 27, 1927.[6] The Government even accepted the obligation to make restitution, according to the directives of Canon Law, of those goods which might be reclaimed from other countries:

Article XXII, 4° : The goods which formerly may have belonged to the Church and which the Republic of Lithuania

[4] The writer's translation. Original text: "La République de Lithuanie reconnait les droits de propriété des personnes juridiques ecclésiastiques et religieuses à tous les biens meubles et immeubles, capitaux, rentes et autres droits, que ces personnes juridiques possèdent actuellement dans le territoire de l'Etat.

2. La République de Lithuanie consent à ce que les droits de propriété susmentionnés, dans le cas ou ils ne seraient pas encore inscrits aux registres hypothécaires ou autres instruments juridiques équivalents, aux noms des personnes juridiques qui les possèdent (Evêchés, Chapitres, Congrégations, Ordres religieux, Séminaires, bénéfices paroissiaux, autres bénéfices, etc.) y soient inscrits, et cela sur une déclaration de l'Ordinaire compétent, certifiée par l'autorité civile compétente."—*AAS,* XIX (1927), 431-432; A. Perugini, *Concordata vigentia,* p. 68.

[5] " . . . que ces personnes juridiques possèdent actuellement. . . . "—*AAS,* XIX (1927), 431.

[6] Cf. V. Meysztowicz, "De Conditione Juridica Ecclesiae in Polonia"—*JP,* XI (1931), 15.

may have reclaimed from other States, shall be restored to her in conformity with Canon Law.[7]

The provision of article XXII is a postulate of justice; it accords with the right of the Church to own property, as expressed in canons 1495 and 1499.

The stipulations of article XXII are in agreement with the Lithuanian Constitution, section 51: "The State shall protect private property." [8]

The Law of Agrarian Reform, Section 12, effective as of April 3, 1922, already had provided that the churches, monasteries and their buildings be restored to those Churches from which they had been confiscated by the Russians.[9]

In Lithuania according to the Law of *Hypothèque,*[10] books of *hypothèque* (books of deeds) were kept under the supervision of the Ministry of Justice. The title to property had to be registered in these books. Such registration constituted first class proof of ownership and entitled the owner to transfer the property and to perform other legal acts.

By the Concordat the Government agreed to enter the titles of all the property of the juridical persons of the Church in these books of official registration; and this was to be done according to the declaration of the Ordinaries. The Church property had to

[7] The writer's translation. Original text: "Les biens que la République de Lithuanie revendiquerait auprès des autres Etats et qui appartenaient jadis à l'Eglise, lui seront restitués conformement au Droit Canon."—*AAS,* XIX (1927), 432.

[8] "Valstybė saugo nuosavybės teisę."—*VŽ,* No. 608 (1938), 239.

[9] "Bažnyčios, vienuolynai ir jų trobesiai grąžinami toms tikybinėms organizacijoms, iš kurių jie Rusų vyriausybės buvo atimti.

Nesant šiame paragrafe paminėtų tikybinių įstaigų ar organizacijų, minėtoji žemė ir trobesiai eina į atatinkamų dvasinių vyresnybių bažnytinį fondą."—*VŽ,* No. 83 (1922), 2.

[10] "Ipotekos Įstatymas. I. Bendrieji dėsniai. §1. Nekilnojamųjų turtų teisėms įrašyti—nuosavybės teisei, daiktinėms teisėms svetimame turte ir įkeitimo teisei—vedamos ipotekos knygos. Šitos vadinamos ipotekinėmis." —*VŽ,* No. 560 (1936), 1.

be entered under the names of the juridical persons of the Church; and this accords with the rule of canon 1495.

The decisions of the Highest Tribunal of Lithuania[11] and the practice of the institutions of the State conformed to article XXII of the Concordat.[12]

2. Subsidies of the State.

From the confiscated capital assets and revenues taken from the property of the Church, the Russian Government paid subsidies to the Catholic Church.[13] After Lithuania regained her independence, part of the confiscated goods were returned to the Church, and the rest remained in th possession of the State.[14]

This was one of the reasons for paying subsidies to the Church. In addition, the Lithuanian clergy performed certain duties which were essential to the State, such as the keeping of records and the submitting of them to the State.[15] Accordingly, justice required that the Lithuanian Government pay subsidies to the Church, and this was guaranteed by the stipulations of the Concordat. Article XXIII states:

> The sums paid by the Republic, according to the norms fixed by the law in force under the names of the dioceses of Samogitia and Seinai and of the Apostolic Administration of

[11] Cf. P. Raulinaitis, "Bažnyčia kaipo Juridinis Asmuo"—*Draugija,* No. 12 (1940), 565-566.

[12] Cf. P. Raulinaitis, "Nekilnojamųjų Turtų Nuosavybės Dokumentų Sutvarkymas"—*Draugija,* No. 2 (1940), 110-111.

[13] Cf. the concordat with Russia in 1847, *Articoli non Concordati,* section 9.—A. Mercati, *Raccolta di Concordati,* p. 764.

[14] Article XXII. 3°, of the Lithuanian Concordat: "La question des biens immeubles dont l'Eglise a été privée par la Russie et qui se trouveraient actuellement en possession de l'Etat lithuanien, sera réglée par un arrangement ultérieur."—*AAS,* XIX (1927), 432; A. Perugini, *Concordata vigentia,* p. 68.

[15] Article XIV of the Concordat—*AAS,* XIX (1927), 429; A. Perugini, *Concordata vigentia,* p. 64. Cf. *supra,* pp. 115 and 116 for the text of this article.

Vilnius, respectively to the Archdiocese of Kaunas, and to the dioceses of Vilkaviškis and Kaišedorys, shall also be paid, and in the same proportion, to the new dioceses of Telšiai and Panevėžys. The State, moreover, binds itself to increase these allotments in the same proportion as it will do so for the other branches of the Administration of State.[16]

The Lithuanian Government even before the Concordat and before the establishment of an ecclesiastical province in Lithuania paid annual subsidies to the former dioceses of Samogitia and Seinai, and to that part of the diocese of Vilnius which was included in Lithuania and was administered by the Apostolic Administrator.[17] By the Concordat the subsidies were extended to all the newly formed dioceses. This provision is in agreement with the principle of ecclesiastical public law, that the Catholic State, as a collective society containing members of the Church, should, if necessary, support the Church by subsidies.[18]

The Lithuanian Government accepted its duty to support the Church.[19] The civil laws, even before the Concordat, regulated

[16] The writer's translation. Original text: "Les sommes. payées par la République conformément aux états fixés par la loi en vigueur sous les noms des diocèses de Samogitie et de Seinai et de l'Administration Apostolique de Vilnius, respectivement a l'archidiocèse de Kaunas et aux diocèses de Vilkaviškis et de Kaišedorys, seront payées aussi et dans la même proportion aux nouveaux diocèses de Telšiai et Panevėžys. L'Etat s'engage toutefois à augmenter ces allocations dans la même proportion qu'il le fera pour les autres branches de l'Administration de l'Etat."—*AAS*, No. XIX (1927), 432; A. Perugini. *Concordata vigentia*, pp. 68-69.

[17] *VŽ*, No. 160 (1924), 3.

[18] A. Ottaviani, *Compendium Iuris Publici Ecclesiastica*, n. 214.

[19] There is a significant provision in the Declaration on the Protection of Minorities in Lithuania. made at Geneva, May 12, 1922: "Article 6. In towns and districts where there is a considerable proportion of Lithuanian nationals belonging to racial, religious or linguistic minorities, these minorities will be assured an equitable share in the enjoyment and application of sums which may be provided out of public funds under the State, municipal or other budgets, for educational, religious or charitable purposes."—M. Hudson, *International Legislation*, II, 871.

If the Churches of minorities are assured of subsidies, it logically follows that the Church of the majority is entitled to more.

State subsidies in the form of salaries to the Bishops, and pastors and the assistant pastors, and in the form of grants to the chancery offices, cathedral chapters, seminaries, and other institutions of the Church.[20] According to a decision of the Cabinet on October 22, 1922, the Church was not held to make a report on the use of her subsidies.[21] These subsidies were paid directly to the Chancery office of each diocese, according to the number of Catholics in that diocese.[22] The budget of the State in 1927 provided 1,376,302 *litas* (about 137,630 dollars) in subsidies to the Catholic Church.[23]

In view of these civil norms the obligations of the State, as resulting from the Concordat, are as follows:

1. To pay subsidies to the five dioceses of Lithuania: Kaunas, Vilkaviškis, Kaišedorys, Telšiai, Panevėžys.

2. To pay subsidies in the amount and manner accepted by the State at the time of the conclusion of the Concordat, that is

a. not less than 1,376,302 litas annually;

b. to be paid directly to the Chancery Offices; and

c. without requiring a report concerning the use of the same.

3. To increase the subsidies to the Church proportionately with the increase of allotments in the other branches of the Administration of the State.[24]

The Government fulfilled the duty which it accepted under the Concordat. In the last budget before the present war (1939) the State provided 1,347,428 *litas* for the Catholic Church in general in Lithuania, and 344,755 *litas* for the Catholic Seminaries.[25]

[20] The Law concerning Salaries of Ecclesiastics.—*VŽ,* No. 32 (1920). 5-6; The Law concerning the Officials of the Institutions of the Church. —*VŽ,* No. 33 (1920, 17-18; Cf. The Laws concerning the Changes of the Salaries of Ecclesiastics.—*VŽ,* No. 112 (1922), 4-5; *VŽ,* No. 160 (1924), 3.

[21] See A. Malakauskis, *Viešosios Bažnytinės Teisės,* p. 164.

[22] A. Malakauskis, *Op. cit.,* p. 164.

[23] Subsidies were paid to other Churches also.—*VŽ,* No. 257 (1926), 14.

[24] Cf. A. Malakauskis, *Viešosios Bažnytinės Teisės,* p. 164.

[25] *VŽ,* No. 701 (1940), 260, 280.

3. Pensions.

Members of the Lithuanian clergy are entitled not only to remuneration from the State, as explained above, but also to pensions. Article XXIV of the Concordat states:

> The Archbishop, the Bishops, the Clergy and the teaching bodies of the major Seminaries shall have a right to a pension. Their participation in the pension fund will be regulated subsequently in agreement with the Ordinaries.[26]

Canon Law favors the paying of pensions to ecclesiastics[27] The civil law also is in accord with the provision of the Concordat concerning pensions. The Lithuanian Constitution has favorable norms concerning State care of the aged [28] and of citizens unable to provide for themselves.[29]

The Law of Pensions and Subsidies [30] provides pensions for the employees of the State. This legislation applies to teachers and employees of private schools if they are recognized by the State.[31] According to this norm, teachers in seminaries already had the right to a pension. The Concordat extends that right to all members of the Lithuanian Clergy, on condition that they pay

[26] The writer's translation. Original text: "L'Archevêque, les Evêques, le Clergé et le corps enseignant dans les grands Séminaires ont droit à la retraite. Leur participation à la caise de retraite sera réglée ultérieurement d'accord avec les Ordinaires."—*AAS,* XIX (1927), 432; A. Perugini, *Concordata vigentia,* p. 69.

[27] Cf. canons 422, 979, 1429.

[28] Section 58: "Valstybė rūpinasi dirbančiaisiais . . . sėnatvės . . . atvejais."—*VŽ,* No. 608 (1938), 240.

[29] Section 59: "Valstybė siekia, kad negalintieji aprūpinti savęs . . . būtų aprūpinti."—*VŽ,* No. 608 (1938), 240.

[30] —*VŽ,* No. 221 (1926), 1-5.

[31] The Rules concerning the Application of the Law of Pensions and Subsidies, section 3: "Pastaba. Šis įstatymas taikomas ir etatiniams ne valdžios laikomų mokyklų mokytojams ir tarnautojams, kurie einant vidurinių ir aukštesnių mokyklų įstatymo § 53 (Vyr. Žin. Nr. 190, eil. Nr. 1284) naudojasi valdžios mokyklų mokytojų ir tarnautojų teisėmis."—*VŽ,* No. 235 (1926), 1.

a certain percentage of their remuneration to the pension fund.[32]

The provision of the Concordat concerning the pensions of the clergy lacked details and was to be determined by new agreements with the Bishops, as provided by article XXIV.

4. Taxes.

In article IV of the Concordat, the State accepted the obligation to help in collecting taxes for the Church from her members. On the other hand, in article XVI, the Church accepts the imposition of taxes on ecclesiastical persons and Church goods for State purposes:

> Ecclesiastics, their goods, and the goods of juridical persons, ecclesiastical and religious, shall be taxable in the same manner as the persons and goods of the citizens of the Republic and of lay juridical persons, with the exception however of edifices consecrated to Divine service, of ecclesiastical Seminaries, of Novitiates of both men and women religious, as well as convents of religious men and women who have taken the vow of poverty, and of the goods and titles whose revenues are destined for the needs of religious worship and do not contribute to the personal income of the beneficiaries. The houses of Bishops and of the parochial clergy, as well as their official premises, shall be treated in the same way as the official houses of the functionaries, and the premises of State institutions.[33]

[32] The Law of Pensions and Subsidies, section 5.—*VŽ,* No. 221 (1926), 5. Cf. P. Malakauskis, *Viešosios Bažnytinės Teisės,* p. 165.

[33] The writer's translation. Original text: "Les ecclésiastiques, leurs biens et les biens des personnes juridiques ecclésiastiques et religieuses, sont imposables a l'égal des personnes et des biens des citoyens de la République et des personnes juridiques laïques, à l'exception toutefois des édifices consacrés au service divin, des Séminaires ecclesiastiques, des maisons de formation des religieux et religieuses de même que des maisons d'habitation des religieux et religieuses, qui ont fait voeu de pauvreté, et des biens et titres dont les revenus sont destinés aux besoins du culte religieux et ne contribuent pas aux revenus personnels des bénéficiaires.

According to this norm the following subjects are taxable: 1. Ecclesiastics for personal taxes; 2. Private property of ecclesiastics; 3. Property of juridical persons of the Church; 4. Property of the monasteries. This is a concession of the Church to the State in view of canons 1530, § 1, n. 3 and 1533.[34]

This concession is made by the Church on two conditions:

1. No special burden of taxes will be imposed on Church property or Church persons over and above the taxes levied on civil persons and civil institutions. The Concordat provides for equality of taxation.

2. By the Concordat an exemption is granted from both local and State taxation on:

a. edifices of public worship;[35] b. seminaries;[36] c. edifices destined for the education of religious (novitiates);[37] d. houses of religious who are bound by the vow of poverty;[38] and e. property and revenues destined for the purpose of public worship.[39] Many of these places are regarded as sacred places[40] and enjoy the privilege of immunity.[41] The exemption, however, is not extended to the personal revenues of the beneficiary.

The habitations of Ordinaries and of the parochial clergy, along with their offices, will be treated by the Fisc in the same manner as the habitations and offices of the officials of State.

Les habitations des Evêques et du Clergé paroissial, de même que leurs locaux officiels, seront traités par le Fisc à l'égal des habitations officielles des fonctionnaires et des locaux des Institutions de l'Etat."—*AAS*, XIX (1927), 430; A. Perugini, *Concordata vigentia*, pp. 65-66.

[34] Cf. A. Ottaviani, "Concordatum Lithuanicum,"—*Apollinaris*, I (1928), 60; A. Blat, *Jus Concordatarium*, p. 149.

[35] Cf. Can. 1161, 1188. In addition to churches and chapels in Lithuania, belfries and similar edifices of the Church enjoy the same privilege. Cf. P. Malakauskis. *Viešosios Bažnytinės Teisės*, p. 160.

[36] Cf. can. 1354.

[37] Cf. can. 554.

[38] Cf. can. 487.

[39] Cf. can. 1255, 1256.

[40] Can. 1154.

[41] Can. 1160.

These exemptions, viewed in the light of the Lithuanian Constitution which proclaim equality under the law,[42] are concessions of the State to the Church.

These concessions, however, are nearly all granted by civil law as well. The Law concerning the Taxation of Land Property exempts cemeteries and the ground on which the church is built (curtilage, close).[43] The Law concerning Taxes on Real Estate in Towns and Cities exempts Church property provided that it is not rented out for profit.[44] However, the Law of Taxation of the Revenue from Labor explicitly states that ecclesiastics have to pay taxes from their personal revenue.[45]

The decision of the Highest Tribunal of Lithuania, on May 4, 1939, concerning the taxation of the institutions of the Church in civil lawsuits by way of government stamps, is in conformity with article XVI of the Concordat.[46]

[42] Section 16.—*VŽ,* No. 608 (1938), 238.

[43] Section 2: "Nuo žemės valstybinio mokesnio atleidžiami . . . b. šventoriai ir kapinės."—*VŽ,* No. 31 (1920), 1; *VŽ,* No. 607 (1938), 230.

[44] Section 3: "Nuo mokesnio atleidžiami . . . tikybinių organizacijų . . . turtai arba jų dalys, kurie neišduodami nuomon pelno tikslu."—*VŽ,* No. 18 (1919), 1; *VŽ,* No. 431 (1933), 4.

[45] Section 1-3.—*VŽ,* No. 388 (1932), 1.

[46] P. Raulinaitis, "Žyminio Mokesnio Reikalavimas Teismuose iš Bažnyčių, Vienuolynų ir Kitų Tikybinių Įstaigų"—*Draugija,* No. 21-22 (1939), 1183.

Chapter XVI

PROBLEMS TO BE SOLVED

1. Revocation of laws which are contrary to the *Concordat*

As a natural consequence of mutual agreement, a stipulation has been made to solve any and all possible collision between the norms of the Concordat and the laws and decrees of both Church and State. Article XXVI declares:

> All the laws, ordinances or decrees which might be in contradiction to the stipulations of the preceding articles shall be *ipso facto* annulled from the moment this present Concordat becomes effective.[1]

This provision is of great value, first of all inasmuch as it proclaims the validity of the norms of the Concordat in internal legislation, and secondly because it gives priority to the stipulations of the Concordat rather than to the norms of internal legislation. In practice, however, the question of abrogated laws and decrees, on account of their contrariety to the provisions of the Concordat, is beset with many difficulties.

First, the discrepancy and contrariety may not always be evident. Again, in certain instances only a part of the law may be contrary to the Concordat's stipulations, and as a result there can arise the question whether the law ceases to be in force in its entirety, or only in part, and how, if the law ceases only in part, the part which remains in force is to be ascertained. Furthermore, even the mere fact of the abrogation of a law can give rise to difficulties when essential legal norms do not accompany the act of abrogation.[2]

[1] The writer's translation. Original text: "Toutes lois, ordonnances ou décrets, qui seraient en contradiction avec les stipulations des articles précédents, seront de ce fait même annulés, dès l'entrée en vigueur du présent Concordat."—*AAS,* XIX (1927), 433; A. Perugini, *Concordata vigentia,* p. 69.

[2] Lacuna et defectum legis.

The Polish Concordat has the same provision,[3] which coincides *verbatim* with that contained in article XXVI of the Lithuanian Concordat. The Polish Government, in the same year that its Concordat was made with the Holy See, by a decree of August 26, 1925[4] published the list of laws which were abrogated by the Concordat.

The Lithuanian Government should also take this necessary step in legislation. Otherwise the different institutions of the country will give her own interpretation, as they did in the past, with regard to which laws in virtue of the Concordat have been abrogated and which have not. Past experience has shown that at times, in consequence of this private form of interpretation, institutions have made conclusions and decisions contrary to their previous judgments.[5]

The preparation of the laws and decrees which are abrogated by the Concordat involves the authentic interpretation of the treaty and should be done with an understanding on the part of the ecclesiastical authorities.[6]

The list of laws and decrees which are abrogated by the Concordat should include all legislation contrary to the stipulations of the agreement, that is, not only the legal enactments of the period before the conclusion of the Concordat, but also the laws and decrees promulgated later.[7]

[3] Article XXV of the Polish Concordat.—*AAS,* XVII (1925), 283; A. Perugini, *Concordata vigentia,* p. 47.

[4] *Monitor Polski,* No. 204 (1925), 1-2.

[5] This actually happened in the case of the Highest Tribunal of Lithuania when it accepted, on October 5, 1936, and on May 3, 1937, two contrary decisions concerning the participation of ecclesiastical juridical persons in civil cases before State tribunals.—Cf. P. Raulinaitis, "Bažnyčia, kaipo Juridinis Asmuo"—*Draugija,* No. 12 (1940), 571.

[6] Cf. G. Gonella, *A World to Reconstruct,* pp. 242-243.

[7] Most contrary to the Concordat are the laws and decrees which are directed against the freedom of the Church in regard to schools, education and Catholic Action, concerning which the writer treated in Part II, Chapter XIII (paragraphs 2, 4, 5) and Chapter XIV of this study.

Another conclusion from article XXVI of the Concordat is the following: there remain in force those laws and decrees which are not contrary to the stipulations of the Concordat, even if they are not mentioned explicitly therein. For example, there remains in force the provision of the Law of Agrarian Reform that the goods of the Catholic Church may be taken only according to the norms of Canon Law.[8] The provision of the Law of Penal Procedure likewise remains in force. According to it, in cases of bigamy brought before the civil court, the fact of bigamy is first to be established by the ecclesiastical tribunal, and only subsequently is the punishment to be inflicted by the court of the State.[9]

Furthermore, there remain in force the norms of the civil law, according to which the cases of Catholics which are concerned with the validity of marriage and with separation, as well as the cases of ecclesiastical persons in regard to ecclesiastical goods, belong to the ecclesiastical tribunals.[10] The norms of the Law of Civil Procedure also remain in force. Accordingly cases concerning the property of married persons, and questions of alimony belong to the civil courts; a certain civil procedure has to be followed to insure the civil rights of legitimated children.[11]

2. The Enlargement of the present Concordat

The Lithuanian Concordat has provisions which indicate the intention of both contracting parties to have new understandings and to enlarge the present stipulations. For example, the norms

[8] The Law of Agrarian Reform, section 13: "Pastaba. Katalikų bažnyčios turtų nusavinimas gali įvykti atsižiūrint į kanonų teises."—*VŽ*, No. 83 (1922), 2.

[9] Law of Criminal Procedure, section 1013.—G. Gronau, *Das litauische Straf-Prozess-Gesetz*, p. 247.

[10] *Сводъ Законовъ*, vol. X, part I, section 72; vol. XI, part I, section 64.

[11] The Law of Civil Procedure, sections 1337, 1345[1], 1460[1-7].—Cf. A. Malakauskis, *Viešosios Bažnytinės Teisės*, p. 167.

concerning patronage seem to be temporary, until a new agreement be made.[12]

The basic principles of the mutual relations between Church and State, however, are elaborated sufficiently in the Lithuanian Concordat, and the provisions concerning the future enlargement of the Concordat, as they are inserted in the text of the agreement, for the most part refer to property rights.

Article XXII, 3°, states:

> The question of the immovable goods of which the Church was deprived by Russia and which now are in the possession of the Lithuanian State, will be regulated by a subsequent arrangement.[13]

This provision indicates first of all, that the Church does not renounce her right to the property which was confiscated by Russia and which was in the possession of the Lithuanian State at the time of the conclusion of the Concordat, and secondly that the Lithuanian Government accepts the obligation not to solve the problem by an unilateral act, but by way of agreement with the Church. This is a postulate of justice and is in agreement with the Lithuanian Constitution, section 51,[14] according to which the State accepts the obligation to protect property.

Another question in the solution of which Lithuania accepted the principle of agreement is that which concerns the goods possessed by foreign ecclesiastical persons:

> Article XXVII. All ecclesiastical goods situated in Lithuania, but belonging to juridic ecclesiastical or religious persons having their seat outside the borders of the Lithuanian

[12] Article XIX: "Le droit de patronage . . . reste en vigueur jusqu'à un nouvel accord."—*AAS,* XIX (1927), 431; A. Perugini, *Concordata vigentia,* p. 67. See Part II, Chapter IX, paragraph 4, of this study.

[13] The writer's translation. Original text: "La question des biens immeubles dont l'Eglise a été privée par la Russie et qui se trouveraient actuellement en possession de l'Etat lithuanien, sera réglée par un arrangement ulterieur."—*AAS,* XIX (1927), 432; A. Perugini, *Concordata vigentia,* p. 68.

[14] *VŽ,* No. 608 (1938), 239.

State, and *vice versa,* shall form the object of a special convention.[15]

The State countenances the principle of subsidies for the maintenance of churches and church buildings and for the construction of new ones. The second part of article XXIII, which has provisions concerning the subsidies of the State to the Church,[16] states:

> A later agreement between the High Contracting Parties will regulate all that concerns the maintenance of churches and other ecclesiastical buildings as well as new constructions demanded for the good of souls.[17]

The State accepts one condition as definitely applicable to that future agreement: the question will be solved according to the exigency of the good of souls.

The Concordat also includes a provision concerning the future understandings between the Bishops and the Government in the matter of the pensions of the clergy.[18]

These, then, are the points for new agreements which are mentioned in the Concordat. It may well be that the changed and changing conditions in the post-war era will bring new material for future stipulations.

[15] The writer's translation. Original text: "Les biens ecclésiastiques situés en Lithuanie, mais appartenant à des personnes juridiques ecclésiastiques et religieuses ayant leur siège hors des frontières de l'Etat lithuanien, et inversement, formeront l'objet d'une convention spéciale."—*AAS,* XIX (1927), 433; A. Perugini, *Concordata vigentia,* p. 70.

[16] See Part II, Chapter XV, paragraph 2. of this study.

[17] "Un accord ultérieur entre les Hautes Parties contractantes réglera tout ce qui regarde le maintien des Eglises et des autres bâtiments ecclésiastiques ainsi que les constructions nouvelles exigées pour le bien des âmes."—*AAS* (1927), 432; A. Perugini, *Concordata vigentia,* p. 69.

[18] Article XXIV. " . . . Leur participation à la caisse de retraite sera réglée ultérieurement d'accord avec les Ordinaires."—*AAS,* XIX (1927), 432; A. Perugini, *Concordata vigentia,* p. 69. Cf. paragraph concerning pensions in this study Part II. Chapter XV, paragraph 3.

CONCLUSIONS

1. The Lithuanian Concordat, historically considered, was largely a result, on the one hand, of the desire of the Holy See to obtain recognition of the basic principles of the new Code of Canon Law in the public life of Lithuania, and, on the other, of the eagerness of the Lithuanian State to provide by peaceful agreement a unified solution of Church affairs in the country, which, upon regaining independence after World War I, inherited three different legal systems.

2. The Lithuanian Concordat incorporates many principles of religious, cultural and ethnical liberty, which predominated in post-war Europe (World War I) and which were accepted in the common public law of the States.

Both High Contracting Parties in this treaty observe their own domain; there is no considerable intruding or mixing of the State in Church affairs or *vice versa*. The canonists and jurists, however, are in agreement that, among the concordats of the era of Pius XI, the Lithuanian Concordat is one of those whose stipulations most closely approximate the principles of ecclesiastical public law and the provisions of the new Code of Canon Law.

3. The stipulations of the Concordat are promulgated by the Lithuanian Government as norms of the civil law of Lithuania. By that transfer of the obligations as accepted in the international agreement into the domain of internal legislation, many provisions of the Code of Canon Law also became in whole or in part the norms of civil law. Such were, for example, the power of jurisdiction of the Church and the right to pursue her end according to the provisions of Canon Law; the moral personality of the Church and of her institutions; the freedom of communication; the protection of the *brachium saeculare*; the privileges of the clergy; the liberty of the Church to make appointments concerning her benefices, offices and institutions; the freedom accorded to Orders, Congregations and Parishes; the norms of Canon Law concerning the right of ecclesiastical moral persons to acquire,

to alienate and to administer property; the full recognition of Church marriage and the right of ecclesiastical tribunals to judge concerning theological and canonical questions involved in marriage cases; the right of the Church to keep records of birth, baptism, marriage, and death, and the recognition of their validity and authority in civil institutions; the immunity of sacred places; the rights of the Church regarding Christian education, and her exercise of these rights over the seminaries, the schools and the societies throughout the country.

4. The Concordat is also a particular Church Law for Lithuania, and through it some norms of the civil law become provisions of ecclesiastical law, as, for example, the right of the civil tribunals, under certain conditions, to judge ecclesiastics in cases of crime; the obligation in certain cases to provide State institutions with the records of birth, marriage, and death; the right of the State to tax certain ecclesiastical property and ecclesiastical persons; the loyalty of the clergy towards the constitutional government, which is guaranteed by the oath of the Bishops, by the *ius praenotificationis* in the appointment of bishops, and by the appointment only of loyal citizens of Lithuania to parochial benefices.

5. The Lithuanian Constitution of 1938, although less favorable to the Church than the two previous Constitutions (1922 and 1928), is, concerning Church affairs, basically in agreement with the stipulations of the Concordat.

6. The civil laws and decrees of Lithuania in the period subsequent to the Concordat up to the first Soviet occupation (1940) are for the most part in conformity with the Concordat. An exception to this conformity is manifest in some of the laws and decrees which bear a relation to Catholic Action, societies, education, and schools.

BIBLIOGRAPHY

Sources

Acta Apostolicae Sedis, Commentarium Officiale, Romae, 1909—

Acta Sanctae Sedis, 41 vols., Romae, 1865-1908.

Annuario Pontificio per l'Anno 1944, Città del Vaticano: Typografia Poliglotta Vaticana, 1944.

Bürgerliches Gesetzbuch vom 18. August 1896 nebst Einführungsgesetz, Berlin: J. Schweitzer Verlag, 1914.

Code Napoléon, édition originale et seule officielle, Paris: L'Imprimerie Impériale, 1810.

Codex Iuris Canonici Pii X Pontificis Maximi iussu digestus, Benedicti Papae XV auctoritate promulgatus, Romae: Typis Polyglottis Vaticanis, 1917.

Codicis Iuris Canonici Fontes cura Emi Petri Card. Gaspari editi, 9 vols., Romae (postea Civitate Vaticana): Typis Polyglottis Vaticanis, 1923-1939. (Vols. VII-IX ed. cura et studio Emi Iustiniani Card. Serédi.)

Conflit Polono-Lithuanien. Question de Vilna. Documents Diplomatique, Kaunas: Ministére des Affaires Étrangères, 1924.

Constitutional Provisions concerning Social and Economic Policy. An international Collection of Texts covering 450 Countries and other Governmental Units, Montreal: International Labor Office, 1944.

Corpus Iuris Canonici, ed. Lipsiensis 2. post Aemilii L. Richteri curas instruxit Aemilius Friedberg, Lipsiae: Ex Officina Bernardi Tauchnitz, 1879-1881. Editio anastatice repetita, Lipsiae: Tauchnitz, 1928.

Corpus Iuris Civilis, 3 vols., ed. Krueger-Mommsen-Schoell-Kroll, Berolini: apud Weidmannos, 1928-1929.

Dailydė, Pranas, *Lietuvos Sutartys su Svetimomis Valstybėmis. Recueil des Traités conclus par la Lithuanie avec les Pays Etrangers,* 2 vols., Kaunas: Užsienių Reikalų Ministerijos leidinys, 1930-1939.

Denzinger, Henr., et Bannwart, Clem., et Umberg, Johan., *Enchiridion Symbolorum, Definitionum et Declarationum de Rebus Fidei et Morum,* 21-23 ed., Friburgi Brisgoviae: Herder, 1937.

[Gronau, G.], *Das litauische Straf-Prozess-Gesetz.* Aus dem Litauischen übersetzt von G. Gronau, Memel: G. Gronau, 1934.

Hardouin, Jean, *Acta Conciliorum et Epistolae Decretales ac Constitutiones Summorum Pontificum,* 12 vols., Parisiis, 1714-1715.

Hudson, Manley O., *International Legislation.* A Collection of the Texts of Multipartite International Instruments of General Interest, 7 vols., covering years 1919-1937 published; further volumes in preparation, Washington, D. C.; Carnegie Endowment for International Peace, 1931—

League of Nations. Treaty Series and International Engagements Registered with the Secretariat of the League of Nations, [Geneva], 1920—

Lietuvos Įstatymai (The Laws of Lithuania), Pirmas Leidinys, Kaunas: A Merkys ir V. Petrulis, 1922.

[Mercati, Angelo,] *Raccolta di Concordati su Materie Ecclesiastiche tra la Santa Sede e le Autorità Civili,* Roma: Tipografia Poliglotta Vaticana, 1919.

Perugini, Angelus, *Concordata Vigentia Notis Historicis et Iuridicis Declarata,* Romae: Pontificium Institutum Utriusque Iuris, 1934.

Piliečių Apsaugos Departamento Aplinkraščių Rinkinys (The Collection of the Circulars of the Department of the Protection of the Citizens), Kaunas: Piliečių Apsaugos Departamentas, 1931.

Principles for Peace, Selections from Papal Documents, Leo XIII to Pius XII, edited for the Bishops' Committee on the Pope's Peace Points, by the Reverend Harry C. Koenig, Washington, D. C.: National Catholic Welfare Conference, 1943.

Pukelevičius, J., *Karinės Prievolės Įstatymas* (The Law of Military Conscription), Kaunas: Neoficialus Piliečių Apsaugos Departamento leidinys, 1931.

Schroeder, Henry J., *Disciplinary Decrees of the General Councils, Text, Translation and Commentary,* St. Louis, Mo.: B. Herder Book Co., 1937.

Собраніе Гражданскихъ Законовъ Губерній Царства Польского, Сапк-Петербургъ: Типографія Второго Отдѣленія Собственной Е. И. В. Канцелярій, 1870.

Statistikos Biuletenis (Bulletin of Statistics), Kaunas: Centralinis Statistikos Biuras, 1924—.

Statistinės Žinios apie Lietuvą ligi Karui 1914 m. (The Statistical Information on Lithuania before the War of 1914), Kaunas: Prekybos ir Pramonės Ministerija, 1919.

Сводъ Законовъ Російской Имперій, томы I-XVI, Санктпетербургъ: Государственная Типографія, 1882-1914.

———, томъ I, часть I: *Сводъ Основныхъ Государственныхъ Законовъ.* Изданіе 1906 года.

———, томъ IX. *Законы о Состояніяхъ.* Изданіе 1899 года.

———, томъ X, гасть I: *Сводъ Законовъ Граждансхихъ и Положеніе о Казенныхъ Порядкахъ и Поставкахъ.* Изданіе 1914 года.

———, томъ XI, гасть I. *Уставъ Духовныхъ Дѣлъ Иностранныхъ*

Вѣроисповѣданій. Изданіе 1896 года.

———, томъ XV. *Уложеніе о Наказаніяхъ Уголовныхъ и Исправительныхъ и Уставъ о Наказаніяхъ, Налагаемыхъ Мировыми Судьями.* Изданіе 1914 года.

Уголовное Уложеніе, Высочайше утвержденное 22 марта 1903 года, С.—Петербургъ: Изданіе Государственной Канцеляріи, 1903.

Vidaus Reikalų Ministerijos Administracijos Departamento aplinkraščiai (The Circulars of the Department of Administration), Kaunas: Vidaus Reikalų Ministerija, 1938.

Vyriausybės Žinios (The News of Government; until June 12, 1920: *Laikinosios Vyriausybės Žinios*), Kaunas, 1918—

Reference Works

Alekna, Antanas, *Katalikų Bažnyčia Lietuvoje* (The History of the Catholic Church in Lithuania). redagavo J. Stakauskas, Kaunas: Šv. Kazimiero Draugijos leidinys, 1936.

Arkivyskupas Jurgis Matulevičius, Marijampolė: Marijonų Spaustuvė, 1933.

Bierbaum, Max, *Das Konkordat in Kultur, Politik und Recht,* Schriften zur deutschen Politik, 19. u. 20. Heft, Freiburg im Breisgau: Herder & Co., 1928.

Bīlmanis, Alfred, *The Baltic States and the Baltic Sea,* Washington, D. C.: Latvian Legation, 1943.

———, *The Baltic States in Post-War Europe,* Washington, D. C.: Latvian Legation, 1944.

Blatt. Albertus, *Ius Concordatarium Postbellicum Conlatum cum Codice Iuris Canonici,* Romae: Apud "Angelicum," 1938.

Cicognani, Amleto G., *Canon Law,* 2. revised edition, authorized English version by Joseph M. O'Hara and Francis Brennan, Philadelphia: The Dolphin Press, 1935.

Činikas, Antanas. *La Réforme Agraire en Lithuanie.* Thèse pour le Doctorat de L'Université de Nancy, Faculté de Droit, Nancy: Imprimerie V. Idoux, 1937.

Concordatum cum Republica Polona 10. II. 1925 anno initum, brevissimo commentario auctum, Włocławek: Biuro Episkopatu Polskiego, 1925.

Consultations de M. A. de Lapradelle, Louis Le Fur et André N. Mandelstam concernant la force obligatoire de la Décision de la Conférence des Ambassadeurs du 15 mars 1923, Paris: Jouve et Cie. 1928.

Dawson, Christopher, *The Judgment of the Nations,* New York: Sheed and Ward, 1942.

Doyle, John J., *Education in Recent Constitutions and Concordats,* The

Catholic University of America. A Dissertation submitted to the Faculty of the Graduate School of Arts and Sciences, Washington. D. C.: The Catholic University of America, 1933.

Eckhardt, Carl C., *The Papacy and World Affairs,* Chicago: The University of Chicago Press, 1937.

Ehret, Joseph, *La Lithuanie,* Genève: Edition Altar. 1919.

Eppstein, John, *The Catholic Tradition of the Law of Nations,* published for the Carnegie Endowment for International Peace, Washington, D. C.: Catholic Association for International Peace, [1935].

Eretas. Juozas, *Suvažiavimo Darbai 1933* (Acts of the Convention of the Catholic Academy of Science), Kaunas: Liet. Kat. Mokslo Akademija, 1935.

Giannini, Amedeo, *I Concordati Postbellici,* Milano: "Vita e Pensiero," 1929.

Gonella, Guido, *A World to Reconstruct,* Pius XII on Peace and Reconstruction, translated by Lincoln Bouscaren, under the auspices of the Bishops' Committee on the Pope's Peace Points, Milwaukee: The Bruce Publishing Company, [1944].

Government Statistical Almanac 1937, The, [Kaunas:] Centralinis Statistikos Biuras [1937].

Graham, Malbone W., Jr., *New Governments of Eastern Europe,* American Political Science Series. New York: Henry Holt and Company [1927].

Graužinis, Casimir, *La Question de Vilna,* Paris: Jouve & Cie, 1927.

Hambro, C. J., *How to Win the Peace,* Philadelphia: J. B. Lippincott Company [1942].

Harrison, E. J., *Lithuania,* London: Hazell. Watson and Viney, LD, 1928.

Hull, Cordell, *Opening Address to the Inter-American Conference for the Maintenance of Peace,* Buenos Aires, Argentina, December 5, 1936, Washington, D. C.: Government Printing Office, 1936.

Janulaitis Augustinas, *Lietuvos Visuomenės ir Teisės Istorija* (The History of Social Life and Law in Lithuania), Tilžė: Švietimo Ministerijos leidinys, 1920.

Jaščenka, A., *Tarptautinės Teisės Kursas* (The International Law), I tomas. Konstitucinė teisė. Kaunas: V. D. Univ. Teisių Fak. leidinys, 1931.

Jusaitis, Antanas, *The History of the Lithuanian Nation and its present National Aspirations,* [Philadelphia] The Lithuanian Catholic Truth Society, 1918.

Kavolis, M., *Bažnytinės Tikybiniai Mišriosios ir Civilinės Moterystės Juridinė Padėtis Lietuvoje* (The Juridical Situation of Mixed and Civil Marriages in Lithuania), Kaunas, 1930.

Kiszling, Helmut, *Abschlusz und Inhalt der neueren Konkordate,* Inaugural—Dissertation zur Erlangung der juristischen Doktorwüde einer Hohen Rechts—und Wirtschaftlichen Facultät (Rechtswissenschaftliche Abteilung) der Eberhard Karls — Universität zu Tübingen, Tübingen: Eugen Göbel, 1931.

Klimas. P., *Der Werdegang des Litauischen Staates von 1915 bis zur Bildung der provisorischen Regierung im November 1918,* Dargestellt auf Grund amtlicher Dokumente, Berlin: Pasz & Garleb G. m. b. H., 1919.

Konkordat Polski ze Stolicą Apostolską, Lwow: Nakładem Tow. "Biblioteka Religijna," 1925.

Konkordatas tarp Šventojo Sosto ir Lietuvos Valdžios (Lithuanian Translation of the Concordat), Chicago: "Draugas," 1928.

La Persécution de L'Eglise en Lithuanie et particulièrment dans le Diocèse de Vilna, traduction du Polonais revue et précédée d'une Préface par Le R. P. Lescoeur, Paris: Ch. Douniol et Cie, 1873.

Le Bideau, Louis P. M., *Les Relations Lithuano-Polonaises,* Thèse pour le Doctorat en Droit, Faculté de Droit, No. 6, Université d'Alger, 1934.

Lietuvos Universitetas. The University of Lithuania, Kaunas: Valstybės Spaustuvė, 1927.

Malakauskis, P., *Viešosios Bažnytinės Teisės* (The Public Law of the Church), Kaunas: V. D. Universiteto Teologijos-Filosofijos Fakulteto leidinys, 1931.

Maser, Leo, *Das Konkordat zwischen dem Apostolischen Stuhle und der Republik Litauen vom 27 September 1927 in rechtsvergleichender Betrachtung,* Inaug.-diss. Köln, Lippstadt in Westfalen: C. J. Laumann, 1931.

Miller, Artur, *Nowa Konstytucja Państwa Litewskiego,* Warszawa: F. Hoesicki, 1930.

Natkevičius, Ladas, *Aspect Politique et Juridique du Différend Polono-Lithuanien,* 4. ed.. Paris: E. Duchemin, 1930.

Norem, Owen J. C., *Timeless Lithuania,* Chicago: Amerlith Press, 1943.

Nusikaltimam Kelti ir Tirti Vadovėlis (The Manual for Investigation and Prosecution of Crimes), Kaunas: Piliečių Apsaugos Departamentas, 1925.

Oregon School Cases, Complete Record, Baltimore: The Belvedere Press, Inc. [1925].

Ottaviani, Alaphridus, *Compendium Iuris Publici Ecclesiastici,* Typis Polyglottis Vaticanis: Pontificium Institutum Utriusque Iuris, 1936.

Pakštas, Kazys, *The Lithuanian Situation,* Chicago: Lithuanian Cultural Institute, 1941.

Parsy, Paul, *Les Concordats Récents, 1914-1935,* Histoire, Analyse, Règles Communes, Thèse pour le Doctorat, Université de Paris, Faculté de Droit, Rodez: Imprimerie G. Subervie [1936].

Perez Mier, Laureano. *Iglesia y Estado Nuevo, Los Concordatos ante el Moderno Derecho Publico,* Madrid: Fax, 1940.

Pijius XI, Marijampolė: Liet. Moterų Kultūros Dr-ja, 1937.

Prunskis, Juozas, *Bolševikų Kalėjime ir Sibiro Ištrėmime* (In the Bolshevistic Jails and in the Exile of Siberia), Chicago: A. Gilis, 1943.

———, *Fifteen "Liquidated" Priests in Lithuania,* Chicago, 1943.

——— and S. Š., *Lietuva Nacių ir Bolševikų Vergijoje* (Lithuania under the Slavery of Nazism and Bolshevism), Chicago: A. L. R. K. Federacijos Chicagos Apskrities Spaudos Sekcijos leidinys No. 1, 1944.

Roberti, Franciscus, *De Delictis et Poenis,* Vol. I, Romae: Libraria Pontificii Instituti Utriusque Iuris, 1938.

Römer, M[ykolas]. *Die Verfassungsreform Litauens vom Jahre 1928,* Quellen und Studien, Abteilung: Recht, 7. Heft, München: Osteuropa-Institut in Breslau, 1930.

Rutenberg, Gregor, *Die baltische Staaten und das Völkerrecht,* Riga: Verlag der Buchh. G. Loeffler, 1928.

Šalkauskis, Stasys, *Sur les Confins de deux Mondes.* Essai Synthétique sur le problème de la Civilisation Nationale en Lithuanie, Berne: Bureau de Presse Lithuanien "Lietuva."

Šapoka, A., *Lietuvos Istorija* (The History of Lithuania), Kaunas: Šv. Ministerijos leidinys, 1936.

Schottlaender, Adolf, *Die geschichtliche Entwicklung des Satzes: Nulla poena sine lege* (Strafrechtliche Abhandlungen, Heft 132, Breslau: Schletter'sche Buchh.. 1911.

Šėmis, B. [M. Biržiška], *Vilniaus Golgota* (Golgotha of Vilnius), Kaunas: Vilniui Vaduoti Sąjunga, 1930.

Senn, Alfred, *The Lithuanian Language,* Chicago: The Lithuanian Cultural Institute, 1942.

Simutis, Anicetas, *The Economic Reconstruction of Lithuania after 1918,* New York: Columbia University Press, 1942.

Speeches and Addresses of Abraham Lincoln, New York: R. K. Haas, Inc.

Sturzo, Don Luigi, *Politics and Morality,* translated by B. Barclay Carter, London: Burns, Oates and Washbourne. 1938.

Thomas Aquinas, *Summa Theologica,* 4 vols. (Vol. 5 in preparation), Ottawa: Impensis Studii Generalis O. Pr., 1941-1944.

Torrubiano Ripoll, Jaime, *Los Concordatos de la Postguerra y la Constitucion Religiosa de los Estados,* Madrid: M. Aguilar, 1931.

Trakiškis, A., *The Situation of the Church and Religious Practices in Occupied Lithuania,* New York: Lithuanian Bulletin, 1944.

Tumas, Juozas, *Vyskupas Valančius. Pastabos Pačiam Sau* (Memoirs of Bishop Valančius), Kaunas: Švietimo Ministerija, 1929.

Turchi, Nicolà, *La Lituania nella Storia e nel Presente,* Roma: Instituto per L'Europa Orientale, 1933.

Verax. Casimiro, *Latuania entre Fuego Cruzado,* Buenos Aires: A. Moly, 1944.

Viscont, Antoine, *La Lithuanie Religieuse,* Paris: G. Crès & Cie, 1918.

Vytauto Didžiojo Universitetas (The University of Vytautas the Great), Kaunas: V. D. Universiteto Kanceliarija, 1933.

Wagnon, Henri, *Concordats et Droit International,* Fondament, Élaboration, Valeur et Cessation du Droit Concordataire. Universitas Catholica Lovaniensis. Dissertationes ad gradum magistri in Facultate Juris Canonici consequendum conscriptae, Series II, Tomus 29, Gembloux: J. Duculot, 1935.

Wright, John J., *National Patriotism in Papal Teaching,* Westminster: The Newman Bookshop, 1943.

Yla, Stasys, *Krikščionybės Įvedimas Lietuvoje,* (The Introduction of Christianity into Lithuania), Kaunas: "Sakalas," 1938.

PERIODICALS

American Journal of International Law, New York, 1907-

Apollinaris, Romae, 1928-

Archiv für katholisches Kirchenrecht, Innsbruck, 1857-1861. Mainz, 1862-

Archivio Giuridico, Bologna, 1868-

Catholic Mind, The, New York, 1903-

Civiltà Cattolica, La, Roma, 1850-

Commentarium pro Religiosis et Missionariis (originally. before 1935, *Commentarium pro Religiosis*), Romae, 1920-

Department of State Bulletin, The, Washington, D. C., 1939-

Draugija, Kaunas, 1937-

Economic and General Bulletin (mimeographed), London, 1924-

Europa Orientale, L', Roma, 1921-

Europe Nouvelle, L', Paris, 1918-

Ganytojas, Kaunas, 1919-1922.

Jus Pontificium, Romae, 1921-

Monitor Polski, Warszawa, 1918-

New York Times, New York, 1851-

Periodica de Re Morali, Canonica, Liturgica (originally *Periodica de Re Canonica et Morali utili praesertim Religiosis et Missionariis*, Brugis, 1905-), Brugis, 1927-1936, Romae, 1937-

Revue de Droit International et de Législation Comparée, Bruxelles. 1869-

Rivista di Diritto Publico, Bologna, 1890-

Rocznik Prawniczy Wilenski, Wilno, 1925-

Švietimo Darbas, Kaunas, 1919-

Švietimo Ministerijos Žinios, Klaipėda, 1931-1933.

Tablet, The, London, 1868-

Tiesos Kelias, Kaunas, 1925-

Zeitschrift für Ostrecht, Berlin, 1927-

Žinių Santrauka (mimeographed), New York, 1944-

Articles

Anonymous, "Les Concordats Lithuanien et Letton"—*L'Europe Nouvelle*, X (1928), 117-118.

———, "The Vilnius Question"—*The Government Statistical Almanac 1937*, pp. 342-363.

Bertola, Arnaldo, "*Attività Concordataria e Codificazione del Diritto della* Chiesa"—*Archivio Giuridico*, CXI (1934), 137-177.

Boosz, ., "Katholische Konkordate und evangelische Kirchenverträge unter besonderer Berücksichtigung des ev. Memelabkommens von 1925"—*Archiv für katholisches Kirchenrecht*, CVII (1927), 33-44.

Cappello, Felix M.. "De Natura Concordatorum"—*JP*, VIII (1928), 15-28, 78-90; IX (1929), 128-140.

Česaitis, Ignas, "Paskutinės Valandos" (The Last Hours)—*Arkivyskupas Jurgis Matulevičius*, pp. 49-52.

De la Brière, Yves, "La Renaissance Contemporaine du Droit Canonique dans plusieurs Législations Séculieres Grâce aux divers Concordats du Pontificat de Pie XI"—*Revue de Droit International et de Législation Comparée*, XVI (1935), 213-245.

Fridstein. V., "Der Einflusz der litauischen Verfassung auf die übernommene russische Gesetzgebung"—*Zeitschrift für Ostrecht*, VI (1932), 567-582.

Gerstmann, Adam, "Na Marginese Konkosdatu"—*Konkordat Polski ze Stolicą Apostolską*, pp. 5-33.

Giannini, Amedeo, "La Costituzione Apostolica *Lituanorum Gente*"—

L'Europa Orientale, VI (1926), 373-378.

———, "La Revisione della Costituzione Lituana"—*L'Europa Orientale*, IX (1929), 399-412.

Goyeneche, Servus, "De Pii Pp XI Operositate Legifera"—*Apollinaris*, XII (1939), 481-489.

Hilling, Nicolaus, "Die Gesetzgebung des Papstes Pius XI"—*Archiv für katholisches Kirchenrecht*, CXIX (1939), 309-351; CXX (1940), 4-32.

Kuraitis, Pranciškus. "Konkordatas Šv. Sosto ir Lietuvos Respublikos" (The Lithuanian Concordat)—*TK*, IV (1928), 35-36.

Labanauskas, J., "Bažnytinės Pareigavietės" (The Ecclesiastical Offices) —*Draugija*, No. 1 (1939), 66-68; No. 2 (1939), 140-144; No. 3 (1939), 218.

Lampis, Giuseppe. "Il Concordato tra la Santa Sede e lo Stato Lituano" —*Rivista di Diritto Publico*, XXI (1929), 227-235.

Meysztowicz, V., "De Conditione Juridica Ecclesiae in Polonia"—*JP*, X (1930), 269-279; XI (1931), 3-19.

Ottaviani, Alafidus, "Concordatum Lithuanicum"—*Apollinaris*, I (1928), 53-64, 140-149.

Prunskis, Juozas, "Pijaus XI Konkortatų Politika" (The Policy of the Concordats of Pius XI)—*Pijus XI*, pp. 285-305.

Raulinaitis, Pranas V., "Bažnyčia Kaipo Juridinis Asmuo" (The Church as a Juridical Person)—*Draugija*, No. 12 (1940), 563-573.

———. "Nekilnojamųjų Turtų Nuosavybės Dokumentų Sutvarkymas" (The Obtaining of the Documents regarding Real Estate)—*Draugija*, No. 2 (1940), 110-111.

———, "Žyminio Mokesnio Reikalavimas Teismuose iš Bažnyčių, Vienuolynų ir kitų Tikybinių Įstaigų" (The Taxes on Ecclesiastical Moral Persons in Lawsuits)—*Draugija*, No. 21-22 (1939), 1183-1184.

Rutenberg, Gregor, "The Baltic States and the Soviet Union"—*American Journal of International Law*, XXIX (1935), 598-615.

Ruzé, Robert, "A Propos des Nouveaux Accords du Saint-Siège: Concordat avec la Lithuanie; *Modus Vivendi* avec la Tchécoslovaquie"—*Revue de Droit International et de Législation Comparée*, X (1939), 336-364.

Schweiger, Petrus, "Jus Religiosorum Concordatum pro Polonia"—*CpR*, VIII (1927), 455-464; IX (1928), 120-126; 341-350; X (1929), 184-192.

Turchi, Nicolà, "La Lituania e il Concordato Polacco"—*L'Europa Orientale*, V (1925), 294-296.

Wilanowski, Boleslaw, "Stosunek Kosciola do Państwa w Swietle Ostatnich Konkordatów"—*Rocznik Prawniczy Wileński,* IV (1930), 107-208.

———, "Ustępstwa ze strony Kościoła na Rzecz Państwa Poczynione w Konkordacie z 10 Lutego 1925 w Swietle Konkordatow innych"—*Rocznik Prawniczy Wilenski,* II (1928), 177-240.

Abbreviations

AAS—Acta Apostolicae Sedis.
ASS—Acta Sanctae Sedis.
CpR—Commentarium pro Religiosis.
JP—Jus Pontificium.
ŠMŽ—Švietimo Ministerijos Žinios.
TK—Tiesos Kelias.
VŽ—Vyriausybės Žinios.

BIOGRAPHICAL NOTE

Joseph Prunskis was born December 22, 1907, in Žvilbučiai, Lithuania. He received his secondary education in Utena and Rokiškis. From 1925 he was principal of the public school of Duliai. He completed his philosophical and theological courses at the University of Kaunas and was ordained to the priesthood in 1932. For two years he was teacher of religion at the public *gymnasium* of Kupiškis. Continuing his postgraduate studies at the University of Kaunas, he received the degree of Licentiate in Canon Law on June 15, 1935. From 1936 until 1939 he was editor of the Catholic daily *XX Amžius* and, later, director of the Catholic Press Bureau in Lithuania. Interested in press activities and in the works of Catholic Action, he visited Austria, Belgium, Canada, Czecho-Slovakia, Estonia, Finland, France, Germany, Hungary, Italy, Latvia, Poland, Portugal, Spain, and Sweden.

When Lithuania was occupied by the Bolsheviks, he had to seek refuge in foreign countries. While in Germany he was held 10 days in a concentration camp. From 1940 to 1944 he was assistant at St. George's parish in Chicago and director of the Lithuanian Catholic Press Bureau in the USA. In October, 1944, he enrolled in the School of Canon Law at the Catholic University of America.

ALPHABETICAL INDEX

CANON LAW STUDIES

1. Freriks, Rev. Celestine A., C.PP.S., J.C.D., Religious Congregations in Their External Relations, 121 pp., 1916.
2. Galliher, Rev. Daniel M., O.P., J.C.D., Canonical Elections, 117 pp., 1917.
3. Borkowski, Rev. Aurelius L., O.F.M., J.C.D., De Confraternitatibus Ecclesiasticis, 136 pp., 1918.
4. Castillo, Rev. Cayo, J.C.D., Disertacion Historico-Canonica sobre la Potestad del Cabildo en Sede Vacante o Impedida del Vicario Capitular, 99 pp., 1919 (1918).
5. Kubelbeck, Rev. William J., S.T.B., J.C.D., The Sacred Pentitentiaria and Its Relations to Faculties of Ordinaries and Priests, 129 pp., 1918.
6. Petrovits, Rev. Joseph J.C., S.T.D., J.C.D., The New Church Law On Matrimony, X-461 pp., 1919.
7. Hickey, Rev. John J., S.T.B., J.C.D., Irregularities and Simple Impediments in the New Code of Canon Law, 100 pp., 1920.
8. Klekotka, Rev. Peter J., S.T.B., J.C.D., Diocesan Consultors, 179 pp., 1920.
9. Wanenmacher, Rev. Francis, J.C.D., The Evidence in Ecclesiastical Procedure Affecting the Marriage Bond, 1920 (Printed 1935).
10. Golden, Rev. Henry Francis, J.C.D., Parochial Benefices in the New Code, IV-119 pp., 1921 (Printed 1925).
11. Koudelka, Rev. Charles J., J.C.D., Pastors, Their Rights and Duties According to the New Code of Canon Law, 211 pp., 1921.
12. Melo, Rev. Antonius, O.F.M., J.C.D., De Exemptione Regularium, X-188 pp., 1921.
13. Schaaf, Rev. Valentine Theodore, O.F.M., S.T.B., J.C.D., The Cloister, X-180 pp., 1921.
14. Burke, Rev. Thomas Joseph, S.T.D., J.C.D., Competence in Ecclesiastical Tribunals, IV-117 pp., 1922.
15. Leech, Rev. George Leo, J.C.D., A Comparative Study of the Constitution, "Apostolicae Sedis" and the "Codex Juris Canonici," 179 pp., 1922.
16. Motry, Rev. Hubert Louis, S.T.D., J.C.D., Diocesan Faculties According to the Code of Canon Law, II-167 pp., 1922.
17. Murphy, Rev. George Lawrence, J.C.D., Delinquencies and Penalties in the Administration and Reception of the Sacraments, IV-121 pp., 1923.

*** Below n. 100 only the following numbers are still available: Nos. 25, 57 and 75. Beginning with n. 100 only the following numbers are unavailable: Nos. 100-111 inclusive, 113 and 115-117 inclusive.**

18. O'Reilly, Rev. John Anthony, S.T.B., J.C.D., Ecclesiastical Sepulture in the New Code of Canon Law, II-129 pp., 1923.
19. Michalicka, Rev. Wenceslas Cyrill, O.S.B., J.C.D., Judicial Procedure in Dismissal of Clerical Exempt Religious, 107 pp., 1923.
20. Dargin, Rev. Edward Vincent, S.T.B., J.C.D., Reserved Cases According to the Code of Canon Law, IV-103, pp., 1924.
21. Godfrey, Rev. John A., S.T.B., J.C.D., The Right of Patronage According to the Code of Canon Law, 153 pp., 1924.
22. Hagedorn, Rev. Francis Edward, J.C.D., General Legislation on Indulgences, II-154 pp., 1924.
23. King, Rev. James Ignatius, J.C.D., The Administration of the Sacraments to Dying Non-Catholics, V-141 pp., 1924.
24. Winslow, Rev. Francis Joseph, A.F.M., J.C.D., Vicars and Prefects Apostolic, IV-149 pp., 1924.
25. Correa, Rev. Jose Servelion, S.T.L., J.C.D., La Potestad Legislativa de la Iglesia Catolica, IV-127 pp., 1925.
26. Dugan, Rev. Henry Francis, A.M., J.C.D., The Judiciary Department of the Diocesan Curia, 87 pp., 1925.
27. Keller, Rev. Charles Frederick, S.T.B., J.C.D., Mass Stipends, 167 pp., 1925.
28. Paschang, Rev. John Linus, J.C.D., The Sacramentals According to the Code of Canon Law, 129 pp., 1925.
29. Piontek, Rev. Cyrillus, O.F.M., S.T.B., J.C.D., De Indulto Exclaustrationis necnon Saecularizationis, XIII-289 pp., 1925.
30. Kearney, Rev. Richard Joseph, S.T.B., J.C.D., Sponsors at Baptism According to the Code of Canon Law, IV-127 pp., 1925.
31. Bartlett, Rev. Chester Joseph, A.M., LL.B., J.C.D., The Tenure of Parochial Property in the United States of America, V-108 pp., 1926.
32. Kilker, Rev. Adrian Jerome, J.C.D., Extreme Unction, V-425 pp., 1926.
33. McCormick, Rev. Robert Emmett, J.C.D., Confessors of Religious, VIII-266 pp., 1926.
34. Miller, Rev. Newton Thomas. J.C.D., Founded Masses According to the Code of Canon Law, VII-93 pp., 1926.
35. Roelker, Rev. Edward G., S.T.D., J.C.D., Principles of Privilege According to the Code of Canon Law, XI-166 pp., 1926.
36. Bakalarczyk, Rev. Richardus, M.I.C., J.U.D., De Novitiatu, VIII-208 pp., 1927.
37. Pizzuti, Rev. Lawrence, O.F.M., J.U.L., De Parochis Religiosis, 1927. (Not printed).
38. Bliley, Rev. Nicholas Martin, O.S.B., J.C.D., Altars According to the Code of Canon Law, XIX-132 pp., 1927.

39. Brown, Mr. Brendan Francis, A.B. LL.M., J.U.D., The Canonical Juristic Personality with Special Reference to Its Status in the United States of America, V-212 pp., 1927.
40. Cavanaugh, Rev. William Thomas, C.P., J.U.D., The Reservation of the Blessed Sacrament, VIII-101 pp., 1927.
41. Doheny, Rev. William J., C.S.C., A.B., J.U.D., Church Property: Modes of Acquisition, X-118 pp., 1927.
42. Feldhaus, Rev. Aloysius H., C.PP.S., J.C.D., Oratories, IX-141 pp., 1927.
43. Kelly, Rev. James Patrick, A.B., J.C.D., The Jurisdiction of the Simple Confessor, X-208 pp., 1927.
44. Neuberger, Rev. Nicholas J., J.C.D., Canon 6 or the Relation of the Codex Juris Canonici to the Preceding Legislation, V-95 pp., 1927.
45. O'Keefe, Rev. Gerald Michael, J.C.D., Matrimonial Dispensations, Powers of Bishops, Priests and Confessors, VIII-232 pp., 1927.
46. Quigley, Rev. Joseph A.M., A.B., J.C.B., Condemned Societies, 139 pp., 1927.
47. Zaplotnik, Rev. Johannes Leo, J.C.D., De Vicariis Foraneis, X-142 pp., 1927.
48. Duskie, Rev. John Aloysius, A.B., J.C.D., The Canonical Status of the Orientals in the United States, VIII-196 pp., 1928.
49. Hyland, Rev. Francis Edward, J.C.D., Excommunication, Its Nature, Historical Development and Effects, VIII-181 pp., 1928.
50. Reinmann, Rev. Gerald Joseph, O.M.C., J.C.D., The Third Order Secular of Saint Francis, 201 pp., 1928.
51. Schenk, Rev. Francis J., J.C.D., The Matrimonial Impediments of Mixed Religion and Disparity of Cult, XVI-318 pp., 1929.
52. Coady, Rev. John Joseph, S.T.D., J.U.D., A.M., The Appointment of Pastors, VIII-150 pp., 1929.
53. Kay, Rev. Thomas Henry, J.C.D., Competence in Matrimonial Procedure, VIII-164 pp., 1929.
54. Turner, Rev. Sidney Joseph, C.P., J.U.D., The Vow of Poverty, XLIX-217 pp., 1929.
55. Kearney, Rev. Raymond, A., A.B., S.T.D., J.C.D., The Principles of Delegation, VII-149 pp., 1929.
56. Conran, Rev. Edward James, A.B., J.C.D., The Interdict, V-163 pp., 1930.
57. O'Neil, Rev. William H., J.C.D., Papal Rescripts of Favor, VII-218 pp., 1930.
58. Bastnagel, Rev. Clement Vincent, J.U.D., The Appointment of Parochial Adjutants and Assistants, XV-257 pp., 1930.
59. Ferry, Rev. William A., A.B., J.C.D., Stole Fees. V-135 pp., 1930.
60. Costello, Rev. John Michael, A.B., J.C.D., Domicile and Quasi-domicile, VII-201 pp., 1930.

61. Kremer, Rev. Michael Nicholas, A.B., S.T.B., J.C.D., Church Support in the United States, VI-1930.
62. Angulo, Rev. Luis, C.M., J.C.D., Legislation de la Iglesia sobre la intencion en la application de la Santa Misa, VII-104 pp., 1931.
63. Frey, Rev. Wolfgang Norbert, O.S.B., A.B., J.C.D., The Act of Religious Profession, VIII-174 pp., 1931.
64. Roberts, Rev. James Brendan, A.B., J.C.D., The Banns of Marriage, XIV-140 pp., 1931.
65. Ryder, Rev. Raymond Aloysius, A.B., J.C.D., Simony, IX-151 pp., 1931.
66. Campagna, Rev. Angelo, Ph.D., J.U.D., Il Vicario Generale del Vescovo, VII-205 pp., 1931.
67. Cox, Rev. Joseph Godfrey, A.B., J.C.D., The Administration of Seminaries, VI-124 pp., 1931.
68. Gregory, Rev. Donald J., J.U.D., The Pauline Privilege, XV-165 pp., 1931.
69. Donohue, Rev. John F., J.C.D., The Impediment of Crime, VII-110 pp., 1931.
70. Dooley, Rev. Eugene A., O.M.I., J.C.D., Church Law On Sacred Relics, IX-143 pp., 1931.
71. Orth, Rev. Raymond Clement, O.M.C., J.C.D., The Approbation of Religious Institutes, 171 pp., 1931.
72. Pernicone, Rev. Joseph M., A.B., J.C.D., The Ecclesiastical Prohibition of Books, XII-267 pp., 1932.
73. Clinton, Rev. Connell, A.B., J.C.D., The Paschal Precept, IX-108 pp., 1932.
74. Donnelly, Rev. Francis B., A.M., S.T.L., J.C.D., The Diocesan Synod, VIII-125 pp., 1932.
75. Torrente, Rev. Camilo, C.M.F., J.C.D., Las Processiones Sagradas, V-145 pp., 1932.
76. Murphy, Rev. Edwin J., C.PP.S., J.C.D., Suspension Ex Informata Conscientia, XI-122, pp., 1932.
77. Mackenzie, Rev. Eric F., A.M., S.T.L., J.C.D., The Delict of Heresy in its Commission, Penalization, Absolution, VII-124 pp., 1932.
78. Lyons Rev. Avitus E., S.T.B., J.C.D., The Collegiate Tribunal of First Instance, XI-147 pp., 1932.
79. Connolly, Rev. Thomas A., J.C.D., Appeals, XI-195 pp., 1932.
80. Sangmeister, Rev. Joseph V., A.B., J.C.D., Force and Fear as Precluding Matrimonial Consent, V-211 pp., 1932.
81. Jaeger, Rev. Leo A., A.B., J.C.D., The Administration of Vacant and Quasi-vacant Episcopal Sees in the United States, IX-229 pp., 1932.
82. Rimlinger, Rev. Herbert T., J.C.D., Error Invalidating Matrimonial Consent, VII-79 pp., 1932.

83. Barrett, Rev. John D.M., S.S., J.C.D., A Comparative Study of the Third Plenary Council of Baltimore and the Code, IX-221 pp., 1932.
84. Carberry, Rev. John J., Ph.D., S.T.D., J.C.D., The Juridical Form of Marriage, X-177 pp., 1934.
85. Dolan, Rev. John L., A.B., J.C.D., The Defensor Vinculi, XII-157 pp., 1934.
86. Hannan, Rev. Jerome D., A.M., S.T.D., LL.B., J.C.D., The Canon Law of Wills, IX-517 pp., 1934.
87. Lemieux, Rev. Delisle A., A.M., J.C.D., The Sentence in Ecclesiastical Procedure, IX-131 pp., 1934.
88. O'Rourke, Rev. James J., A.B., J.C.D., Parish Registers, VII-109 pp., 1934.
89. Timlin, Rev. Bartholomew, O.F.M., A.M., J.C.D., Conditional Matrimonial Consent, X-381 pp., 1934.
90. Wahl, Rev. Francis X., A.B., J.C.D., The Matrimonial Impediments of Consanguinity and Affinity, VI-125 pp., 1934.
91. White, Rev. Robert J., A.B., LL.B., S.T.B., J.C.D., Canonical Ante-Nuptial Promises and the Civil Law, VI-152 pp., 1934.
92. Herrera, Rev. Antonio Parra, O.C.D., J.C.D., Legislation Ecclesiastica sobra el Ayuno y la Abstinencia, XI-191 pp., 1935.
93. Kennedy, Rev. Edwin J., J.C.D., The Special Matrimonial Process in Cases of Evident Nullity, X-165 pp., 1935.
94. Manning, Rev. John J., A.B., J.C.D., Presumption of Law in Matrimonial Procedure, XI-111 pp., 1935.
95. Moeder, Rev. John M., J.C.D., The Proper Bishop for Ordination and Dismissorial Letters, VII-135 pp., 1935.
96. O'Mara, Rev. William A., A.B., J.C.D., Canonical Causes For Matrimonial Dispensations, IX-155 pp., 1935.
97. Reilly, Rev. Peter, J.C.D., Residence of Pastors, IX-81 pp., 1935.
98. Smith, Rev. Mariner T., O.P., S.T.L., J.C.D., The Penal Law For Religious, VII-169 pp., 1935.
99. Whalen, Rev. Donald W., A.M., J.C.D., The Value of Testimonial Evidence in Matrimonial Procedure, XIII-297 pp., 1935.
100. Cleary, Rev. Joseph F., J.C.D., Canonical Limitations on the Alienation of Church Property, VIII-141 pp., 1936.
101. Glynn, Rev. John C., J.C.D., The Promoter of Justice, XX-337 pp., 1936.
102. Brennan, Rev. James H., S.S., A.M., S.T.B., J.C.D., The Simple Convalidation of Marriage, VI-135 pp, 1937.
103. Brunini, Rev. Joseph Bernard, J.C.D., The Clerical Obligations of Canons, 139 and 142, X-121 pp., 1937.
104. Connor, Rev. Maurice, A.B., J.C.D., The Administrative Removal of Pastors, VIII-159 pp., 1937.
105. Guilfoyle, Rev. Merlin Joseph, J.C.D., Custom, XI-144 pp., 1937.

106. Hughes, Rev. James Austin, A.B., A.M., J.C.D., Witnesses in Criminal Trials of Clerics, IX-140 pp., 1937.
107. Jansen, Rev. Raymond J., A.B., S.T.L., J.C.D., Canonical Provisions for Catechetical Instruction, VII-153 pp., 1937.
108. Kealy, Rev. John James, A.B., J.C.D,, The Introductory Libellus in Church Court Procedure, XI-121 pp., 1937.
109. McManus, Rev. James Edward, C.SS.R., J.C.D., The Administration of Temporal Goods in Religious Institutes, XVI-196 pp., 1937.
110. Moriarty, Rev. Eugene James, J.C.D., Oaths in Ecclesiastical Courts, X-115 pp., 1937.
111. Rainer, Rev. Eligius George, C.SS.R., J.C.D., Suspension of Clerics, XVII-249 pp., 1937.
112. Reilly, Rev. Thomas F., C.SS.R., J.C.D., Visitation of Religious, VI-195 pp., 1938.
113. Moriarty, Rev. Francis E., C.SS.R., J.C.D., The Extraordinary Absolution from Censures, XV-334 pp., 1938.
114. Connolly, Rev. Nicholas P., J.C.D., The Canonical Erection of Parishes, X-132 pp., 1938.
115. Donovan, Rev. James Joseph, J.C.D., The Pastor's Obligation in Prenuptial Investigation, VII-322 pp., 1938.
116. Harrigan, Rev. Robert J., M.A., S.T.B., J.C.D., The Radical Sanation of Invalid Marriages, VIII-208 pp., 1938.
117. Boffa, Rev. Conrad Humbert, J.C.D., Canonical Provisions for Catholic Schools, VII-211 pp., 1939.
118. Parsons, Rev. Anscar John, O.M. Cap., J.C.D., Canonical Elections, XII-236 pp., 1939.
119. Reilly, Rev. Edward Michael, A.B., J.C.D., The General Norms of Dispensation, X-156 pp., 1939.
120. Ryan, Rev. Gerald Aloysius, A.B., J.C.D., Principles of Episcopal Jurisdiction, XII-172 pp., 1939.
121. Burton, Rev. Francis James, C.S.C., A.B., J.C.D., A Commentary on Canon 1125, X-222 pp., 1940.
122. Miaskiewicz, Rev. Francis Sigismund, J.C.D., Supplied Jurisdiction according to Canon 209, XII-340 pp., 1940.
123. Rice, Rev. Patrick William, A.B., J.C.D., Proof of Death in Prenuptial Investigation, VIII-156 pp., 1940.
124. Anglin, Rev. Thomas Francis, M.S., J.C.D., The Eucharistic Fast, VIII-183 pp., 1941.
125. Coleman, Rev. John Jerome, J.C.D., The Minister of Confirmation, VI-153 pp., 1941.
126. Downs, Rev. John Emmanuel, A.B., J.C.D., The Concept of Clerical Immunity, XI-163 pp., 1941.

127. Esswein, Rev. Anthony Albert, J.C.D., Extrajudicial Penal Powers of Ecclesiastical Superiors, X-144 pp., 1941.
128. Farrell, Rev. Benjamin Francis, M.A., S.T.L., J.C.D., The Rights and Duties of the Local Ordinary Regarding Congregations of Women Religious of Pontifical Approval, V-195 pp., 1941.
129. Feeney, Rev. Thomas John, A.B., S.T.L., J.C.D., Restitution in Integrum, VI-169 pp., 1941.
130. Findlay, Rev. Stephen William, O.S.B., A.B., J.C.D., Canonical Norms Governing the Deposition and Degradation of Clerics, XVII-279 pp., 1941.
131. Goodwine, Rev. John, A.B., S.T.L., J.C.D., The Right of the Church to Acquire Property, VIII-119 pp., 1941.
132. Heston, Rev. Edward Louis, C.S.C., PhD., S.T.D., J.C.D., The Alienation of Church Property in the United States, XII-222 pp., 1941.
133. Hogan, Rev. James John, S.T.L., J.C.D., Judicial Advocates and Procurators, VIII-200 pp., 1941.
134. Kealy, Rev. Thomas M. A.B., Litt.B., J.C.D., Dowry of Women Religious, IX-152 pp., 1941.
135. Keene, Rev. Michael James, O.S.B., J.C.D., Religious Ordinaries and Canon 198, V-164 pp., 1942.
136. Kerin, Rev. Charles A., S.S., M.A., S.T.B., J.C.D., The Privation of Christian Burial, XVI-279 pp., 1941.
137. Louis, Rev. William Francis, M.A., J.C.D., Diocesan Archives, X-101 pp., 1941.
138. McDevitt, Rev. Gilbert Joseph, A.B., J.C.D., Legitimacy and Legitimation, X-247 pp., 1941.
139. McDonough, Rev. Thomas Joseph, A.B., J.C.D., Apostolic Administrators, X-217 pp., 1941.
140. Meier, Rev. Carl Anthony, A.B., J.C.D., Penal Administrative Procedure Against Negligent Pastors, XI-240 pp., 1941.
141. Schmidt, Rev. John Rogg, A.B., J.C.D., The Principles of Authentic Interpretation in Canon 17 of the Code of Canon Law, XII-331 pp., 1941.
142. Slafkosky, Rev. Andrew Leonard, A.B., J.C.D., The Canonical Episcopal Visitation of the Diocese, X-197 pp., 1941.
143. Swoboda, Rev. Innocent Robert, O.F.M., J.C.D., Ignorance in Relation to the Imputability of Delicts, IX-271 pp., 1941.
144. Dubé, Rev. Arthur Joseph, A.B., J.C.D., The General Principles for the Reckoning of Time in Canon Law. VIII-299 pp., 1941.
145. McBride, Rev. James T., A.B., J.C.D., Incardination and Excardination of Seculars., XX-585 pp., 1941.
146. Król, Rev. John J., J.C.L., The Defendant in Contentious Trials, IX-207 pp., 1942.

147. Comyns, Rev. Joseph J., C.SS.R., J.C.L., The Papal and Episcopal Administration of Church Property, XIV-155 pp., 1942.
148. Barry, Rev. Garrett Francis, O.M.I., J.C.L., Violation of the Cloister, XII-260 pp., 1942.
149. Bolduc, Rev. Gatien, C.S.V., A.B., S.T.L., J.C.L., Les études dans les religions cléricales, VIII-155 pp., 1942.
150. Boyle, Rev. David John, M.A., J.C.L., The Juridic Effects of Moral Certitude on Pre-Nuptial Guarantees, XII-188 pp., 1942.
151. Canavan, Rev. Walter Joseph, M.A., Litt.D., J.C.L., Profession of Faith, XII-143 pp., 1942.
152. Desrochers, Rev. Bruno, A.B., Ph.L., S.T.B., J.C.L., Le Premier Concile Plénier de Québec et le Code de Droit Canonique, XIV-186 pp., 1942.
153. Dillon, Rev. Robert Edward, A.B., J.C.L., Common Law Marriage, X-148 pp., 1942.
154. Dodwell, Rev. Edward John, Ph.D., S.T.B., J.C.L., The Time and Place for the Celebration of Marriage, X-156 pp., 1942.
155. Donnellan, Rev. Thomas Andrew, A.B., J.C.L., The Obligation of the Missa pro Populo, VII-131 pp., 1942.
156. Eltz, Rev. Rev. Louis Anthony, A.B., J.C.D., Cooperation in Crime. XII-208 pp., 1942.
157. Gass, Rev. Sylvester Francis, M.A., J.C.L., Ecclesiastical Pensions, XI-206 pp., 1942.
158. Guiniven, Rev. John Joseph, C.SS.R., J.C.L., The Precept of Hearing Mass on Sundays and Holy Days of Obligation, X-126 pp., 1942.
159. Gulczynski, Rev. John Theophilus, J.C.L., The Desecration and Violation of Churches, X-126 pp., 1942.
160. Hammill, Rev. John Leo, M.A., J.C.L., The Obligations of the Traveler according to Canon 14, VIII-204 pp., 1942.
161. Haydt, Rev. John Joseph, A.B., J.C.L., Reserved Benefices, XI-148 pp., 1942.
162. Huser, Rev. Roger John, O.F.M., A.B., J.C.L., The Crime of Abortion in Canon Law, XII-187 pp., 1942.
163. Kearney, Rev. Francis Patrick, A.B., S.T.L., J.C.L., The Principles of Canon 1127.
164. Linahen, Rev. Leo James, S.T.L., J.C.L., De Absolutione Complicis in Peccato Turpi, 114 pp., 1942.
165. McCloskey, Rev. Joseph Aloysius, A.B., J.C.L., The Subject of Ecclesiastical Law according to Canon 12, XVII-216 pp., 1942.
166. O'Neill, Rev. Francis Joseph, C.SS.R., J.C.L., The Dismissal of Religious in Temporary Vows, XIII-220 pp., 1942.
167. Prince, Rev. John Edward, A.B., S.T.B., J.C.L., The Diocesan Chancellor, X-136 pp., 1942.

168. Riesner, Rev. Albert Joseph, C.SS.R., J.C.L., Apostates and Fugitives from Religious Institutes, IX-168 pp., 1942.
169. Stenger, Rev. Joseph Bernard, J.C.L., The Mortgaging of Church Property, 186 pp., 1942.
170. Waldron, Rev. Joseph Francis, A.B., J.C.L. The Minister of Baptism, XII-197 pp., 1942.
171. Willett, Rev. Robert Albert, J.C.L., The Probative Value of Documents in Ecclesiastical Trials, X-124 pp., 1942.
172. Woeber, Rev. Edward Martin, M.A., J.C.L., The Interpellations, XII-161 pp., 1942.
173. Benko, Rev. Matthew Aloysius, O.S.B., M.A., J.C.D., The Abbot *Nullius*, XVI-148 pp., 1943.
174. Christ, Rev. Joseph James, M.A., S.T.L., J.C.D., Dispensation from Vindictive Penalties, XIV-285 pp. 1943.
175. Clancy, Rev. Patrick, M.. J., O.P., A.B., S.T.Lr., J.C.D., The Local Religious Superior, X-229 pp., 1943.
176. Clarke, Rev. Thomas James, J.C.D., Parish Societies, XII-147 pp., 1943.
177. Connolly, Rev. John Patrick, S.T.L., J.C.D., Synodal Examiners and Parish Priest Consultors, X-223 pp., 1943.
178. Drumm, Rev. William Martin, A.B., J.C.D., Hospital Chaplains, XII-175 pp., 1943.
179. Flanagan, Rev. Bernard Joseph, A.B., S.T.L., J.C.D., The Canonical Erection of Religious Houses, X-147 pp., 1943.
180. Kelleher, Rev. Stephen Joseph, A.B., S.T.B., J.C.D., Discussions with non-Catholics: Canonical Legislation, X-93 pp., 1943.
181. Lewis, Rev. Gordian, C.P., J.C.D., Chapters in Religious Institutes, XII-169 pp., 1943.
182. Marx, Rev. Adolph, J.C.D., The Declaration of Nullity of Marriages Contracted Outside the Church, X-151 pp., 1943.
183. Matulenas, Rev. Raymond Anthony, O.S.B., A.B., J.C.D., Communication, a Source of Privileges, XII-225 pp., 1943.
184. O'Leary, Rev. Charles Gerard, C.SS.R., J.C.D., Religious Dismissed After Perpetual Profession, X-213 pp., 1943.
185. Power, Rev. Cornelius Michael, J.C.D., The Blessing of Cemeteries, XII-213 pp., 1943.
186. Shuhler, Rev. Ralph Vincent, O.S.A., J.C.D., Privileges of Regulars Absolve and Dispense, XII-195 pp., 1943.
187. Ziolkowski, Rev. Thaddeus Stanislaus, A.B., J.C.D., The Consecration and Blessing of Churches, XII-151 pp., 1943.
188. Heneghan, Rev. John Joseph, S.T.D., J.C.D., The Marriages of Unworthy Catholics: Canons 1065 and 1066, XVI-213 pp., 1944.

189. Carroll, Rev. Coleman Francis, M.A., S.T.L., J.C.L., Charitable Institutions.
190. Ciesluk, Rev. Joseph Edward, Ph.B., S.T.L., J.C.L., National Parishes in the United States.
191. Coburn, Rev., Vincent Paul, A.B., J.C.D., Marriages of Conscience, XII-172 pp., 1944.
192. Connors, Rev. Charles Paul, C.S.Sp., A.B., J.C.D., Extra-Judicial Procurators in the Code of Canon Law, X-94 pp., 1944.
193. Coyle, Rev. Paul Raymond, A.B., J.C.L., Judicial Exceptions.
194. Fair, Rev. Bartholomew Francis, A.B., S.T.L., J.C.L., The Impediment of Abduction.
195. Gallagher, Rev. Thomas Raphael, O.P., A.B., S.T.Lr., J.C.D., The Examination of the Qualities of the Ordinand, X-166 pp., 1944.
196. Gannon, Rev. John Mark, S.T.L., J.C.D., The Interstices Required for the Promotion to Orders, XII-100 pp., 1944.
197. Goldsmith, Rev. J. William, B.C.S., S.T.L., J.C.D., The Competence of Church and State over Marriage—Disputed Points, X-128 pp., 1944.
198. Goodwine, Rev. Joseph Gerard, A.B., S.T.B., J.C.D., The Reception of Converts, XIV-326 pp., 1944.
199. Kowalski, Rev. Romuald Eugene, O.F.M., A.B., J.C.D., Sustenance of Religious Houses of Regulars, X-174 pp., 1944.
200. McCoy, Rev. Alan Edward, O.F.M., J.C.D., Force and Fear in Relation to Delictual Imputability and Penal Responsibility, XII-160 pp., 1944.
201. McDevitt, Rev. Vincent John, Ph.B., S.T.L., J.C.L., Perjury.
202 Martin, Rev. Thomas Owen, Ph.D., S.T.D., J.C.D., Adverse Possession, Prescription and Limitation of Actions: The Canonical "Praescriptio." XX-208 pp., 1944.
203. Miklosovic, Rev. Paul John, A.B., J.C.L., Attempted Marriages and Their Consequent Juridic Effects.
204. Mundy, Rev. Thomas Maurice, A.B., S.T.L., J.C.L., The Union of Parishes.
205. O'Dea, Rev. John Coyle, A.B., J.C.D., The Matrimonial Impediment of Nonage, VIII-126 pp., 1944.
206. Olalia, Aev. Alexander Ayson, S.T.L., J.C.D., A Comparative Study of the Christian Constitution of States and the Constitution of the Philippine Commonwealth, XII-136 pp., 1944.
207. Poisson, Rev. Pierre-Marie, C.S.C., A.B., Ph.L., Th.L., J.C.L., Droits Patrimoniaux des Maisons et des Églises Religieuses.
208. Stadalnikas, Rev. Casmir Joseph, M.I.C., J.C.D., Reservation of Censures, X-141 pp., 1944.

209. Sullivan, Rev. Eugene Henry, S.T.L., J.C.L., Proof of the Reception of the Sacraments.
210. Vaughan, Rev. William Edward, J.C.D., Constitutions for Diocesan Courts, X-210 pp., 1944.
211. Paro, Rev. Gino, S.T.D., J.C.L., The Right of Apostolic Delegation.
212. Balzer, Rev. Ralph Francis, C.P., J.C.L., The Computation of Time in a Canonical Novitiate.
213. Dougherty, Rev. John Whelan, O.B., S.T.L., J.C.L., De Inquisitione Speciali.
214. Dziob, Rev. Michael Walter, J.C.L., The Sacred Congregation for the Oriental Church.
215. Eidenschink, Rev. John Albert, O.S.B., B.A., J.C.L., The Election of Bishops in The Letters of Pope Gregory the Great.
216. Gill, Rev. Nicholas, C.P., J.C.L., The Spiritual Prefect in Clerical Religious Houses of Study.
217. Hynes, Rev. Harry Gerard, S.T.L., J.C.L., The Privileges of Cardinals.
218. McDevitt, Rev. Gerald Vincent, S.T.L., J.C.L., The Renunciation of an Ecclesiastical Office.
219. Manning, Rev. Joseph Leroy, J.C.L., The Free Conferral of Offices.
220. Meyer, Rev. Louis G., O.S.B., A.B., S.T.B., J.C.L., Alms-gathering by Religious.
221. O'Donnell, Rev. Cletus Francis, M.A., J.C.L., The Marriages of Minors.
222. Prunskis, Rev. Joseph, J.C.L., Comparative Law, Ecclesiastical and Civil, in Lithuanian Concordat.
223. Sweeney, Rev. Francis Patrick, C.Ss.R., J.C.L., The Reduction of Clerics to the Lay State.
224. Vogelpohl, Rev. Henry John, J.C.L., The Simple Impediments to Holy Orders.

www.ingramcontent.com/pod-product-compliance
Lightning Source LLC
LaVergne TN
LVHW050226080826
844660LV00012B/480

* 9 7 8 0 8 1 3 2 2 4 0 6 0 *